Robert
LENKIEWICZ
THE ARTIST AND THE MAN

KEITH NICHOLS

With contributions by:

Louise Courtnell • Lord St Germans • John Lenkiewicz

Robert Lenkiewicz • Michael Palmer

HALSGROVE

First published in Great Britain in 2005

Copyright © 2005 Keith Nichols
Copyright © on individual artworks remains with the Estate of the late Robert Lenkiewicz
Copyright © on all other images remains with those named in this work

All rights reserved. No part of this publication may be reproduced,
stored in a retrieval system, or transmitted in any form or by any means
without the prior permission of the copyright holder.

British Library Cataloguing-in-Publication Data
A CIP record for this title is available from the British Library

ISBN 1 84114 457 6

HALSGROVE
Halsgrove House, Lower Moor Way, Tiverton EX16 6SS
T: 01884 243242 F: 01884 243325
e: sales@halsgrove.com w: www.halsgrove.com

Designed by Karen Binaccioni

Printed and bound by D'Auria Industrie Grafiche Spa, Italy

Contents

Acknowledgements	4
Foreword	5
Introduction	7
Robert Lenkiewicz as a Presence	12
Robert as a Man – A Portrait in Words	32
Robert Lenkiewicz: A Memoir – *Lord St Germans*	69
Robert and the Authorities – A Happening at Plymouth Museum	86
Lenkiewicz as a Painter	91
Robert Lenkiewicz as a Teacher and Painter – *Louise Courtnell*	103
The Painter's Studio	109
The Experience of Being Painted by Lenkiewicz	119
Robert and Women	124
Towards an Understanding	135
Early Influences – *Interview with John Lenkiewicz*	143
Robert and Illness, Robert and Death – *with Michael Palmer*	152
The End of the Show	162

Acknowledgements

It sounds rather trite to open with, 'Without the help of my wife, Lorna, this book would never have been completed'. Embarrassingly, this is not far from the truth. I am not that given to systematic organisation or the rigorous editing of text, whereas she is. Lorna has been an exceptional help with the construction of the book.

It has also been of great value to have had the resource of frequent meetings with Annie Hill-Smith and Yana Trevail. They have provided history, details and views concerning Robert's past and work.

There are four people who have provided major contributions – John Lenkiewicz, Lord St Germans, Louise Courtnell and Michael Palmer. It is very pleasing indeed to have their material. I am also grateful to Sally Moore, Nichola Harry, Ray Balkwill, James Lake, Simon Butler, Irena Boobyer and Dave Goodwin who took the trouble to provide their views on Robert Lenkiewicz as a painter. Lastly, my thanks to Peter Walmsley, executor of the Lenkiewicz estate, to Andy Jones and to Noel Chanan whose generosity with additional photographs is gratefully acknowledged.

Foreword

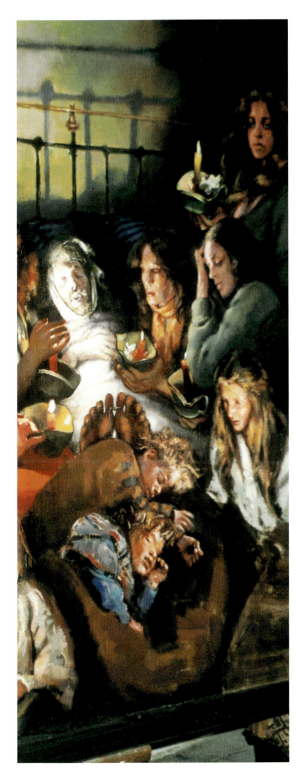

The life of Robert Lenkiewicz is truly a phenomenon. No other painter in modern times has disturbed the public with quite the bewilderment or panache that R O Lenkiewicz achieved. For all who came into contact with him or his paintings few can say that it was not a memorable meeting. Yet, as the author of this book shows, each encounter resulted in distinct and different reactions. As many loved him as disliked him. As many liked his paintings as loathed them.

We who look upon a dead artist's life and work, strive to place the fragments that remain into a mosaic that itself becomes an image we recognise. We are desperate for things to make sense. We ask for light to be thrown even where darkness prevails.

From the early days of discussing this work with Keith Nichols I loftily suggested he write a book that would unravel the apparent enigma that was Lenkiewicz, the man and the artist. Though a personal plea I knew that many others would want what I did, a thread to guide me through the elaborately self-constructed labyrinth of this artist's life.

Here then is that thread – it leads us towards the light.

Simon Butler
The Publisher

August 6th 2002

'Keith, its Yana.'

'Yana, – Hi!'

'Keith, in case you haven't heard I'm calling
with some dreadful news – Robert died yesterday.'

Introduction

This book is best regarded as both an affectionate memorial to Robert Lenkiewicz together with an analysis of certain aspects of his life, work and psychology. It is not a biography as such but rather a look at the man as I and certain others knew him personally. I have included an assembly of comments on his painting from various sources and also make an assessment of the man from the perspective of the professional clinical psychologist.

Having spent many hours in his company in recent years I became very fond of Robert. I cannot claim, though, to have been part of the inner core of devotees who gave so much of their life and time in service of his needs. Hopefully that is an advantage in preparing this text since it makes objectivity less of a challenge and allows critical perspectives alongside the acclamations.

I met Robert Lenkiewicz in the autumn of 1996. Like many events in life it was more by accident than design but he was such a different, powerful and compelling figure that, as with so many of his acquaintances and friends I suppose, meeting with him became something of an addiction. This is ironic in that he talked, wrote and painted on the theme of relationships being nothing more than physiological addictions. Certainly, some of the trail of 'casualties' (usually female) that he left behind in his life seemed to suffer consequences rather like the physiological impact of withdrawal symptoms. Not surprisingly, his death had that effect too. It left some of the key figures in his life bereft – they had, after all, literally given a significant proportion of their lives to him.

We met once every month or so since our first meeting in 1996. I would visit him in his Barbican studio, his cottage in Plymouth, at a weekend cottage he used near Newton Ferrers called Mudbank, in his Basement studio, in St Saviours Church Building where his philosophy library was housed and, more recently, in his new studio and intended gallery in Castle Dyke, Plymouth. This was the so-called Theology Building since it was to house his collection of books on that theme. We also spent an amount of time in various cafés in the Barbican area and, at times, in Derriford Hospital. I would record the content and character of these visits in note form after each event. This was another irony, calculated in this instance. My notes became a standing joke between us since the habit was a direct imitation of the routine by which he had his female sitters record their thoughts and experiences when the

Robert, Anna Navas and the author at Mudbank.

Discussion at Mudbank.

At the Basement studio.

painting gave way to sexual encounter. These notes and sketches compiled both by Robert and the female sitters were the 'aesthetic notes' that formed the basis of his lifelong project on sexual experiences. They also offered a rationalisation for his remarkably prolific 'career' in sexual activity, the scale of which leaves most of us stunned. Throughout this book I will refer to my notes compiled on specific visits, sometimes presenting them as originally written up in the hours after a visit.

After a few months or so of contact I began to realise that Robert was a very unusual and very exceptional man, and that a more serious effort at creating a record was called for, ideally in the form of a book. I also felt that I needed a more weighty rationale to justify taking his time. So, the plan to convert my endeavours into preparing a book rather than just visiting him to talk emerged. I wrote a couple of sample pieces and gave them to Robert. He seemed pleased with the idea and, thus, around May 1998, it became a recognised arrangement between us – I was to write a book on him as both friend and psychologist. He allowed me access to his studios, his home, some of his thoughts, plans and creative leaps, his preparatory sketches and writings prior to a significant painting and, lastly, to some of the research notes from sexual encounters and relationships with women. It was accepted that whenever we met or whatever we looked at my camera was there too.

My background as a clinical psychologist working in coronary rehabilitation provided a third ironic slant to this improbable encounter since, shortly before I met Robert, he underwent coronary bypass surgery and then very slowly deteriorated in health with advancing heart failure. To me he was a classic coronary-prone personality. This set of traits both gave him the persistent drive and vitality to be the giant of creativity that he became and, I believe, eventually contributed to his early death. A little of our conversation involved me trying to persuade him to improve his own general health care.

I have often been asked if I had a treatment role with Robert. Certainly he seemed quietly pleased to have the interest of a psychologist, but was not keen on professional inquiry. I therefore kept things informal and we drifted into being friends rather than client and therapist. In fact, nothing like therapy ever took place although I did occasionally berate him on the health hazards inherent in his lifestyle and the need to ease up if he were to avoid an early death. On such occasions Robert smiled in a distant way, looked over my shoulder and signalled total disinterest with this theme. Alarmingly at times, he gave the impression that he believed me be a psychologist of international eminence. I never disabused him of this erroneous belief.

At Prete's Café, The Barbican.

Sometimes when I have talked to the people who were close to Robert there is the sense that they feel they knew the 'real' Robert in a special, deep and private way. This was probably not truly possible since he presented different faces to different people and, as a lifelong quest, worked at compartmentalising his life and keeping knowledge of his different parts fragmented. His aim, perhaps, was that no one should know the whole version; that was a secret just for him. Curiously, the closer he was to certain key figures in his life the harder he worked at hiding things from them, as will emerge later in this book. He took an apparent lifelong stance against long-term, binding relationships with women. It was something of a paradox, therefore, that Robert had a curious power to evoke possessiveness in people. This seemed to fuel a need to be 'special' to him and, thus, feel that one had special knowledge of him. But it has to be remembered that our perception of people and the world in general is a well-crafted illusory trick. When it comes down to it human perception is simply an act of continual creative construction. The product is 'seeing and knowing' but often these experiences are based on quite insubstantial or incomplete bits of information. Even so, it gives the illusion of knowing. As hinted, people who were close to Robert sometimes talk as if they were the ones who knew him in special depth. But talk to each of them in detail and they regularly contradict one another – differing pictures emerge. This is the effect of his habit of managing his life so that different people knew different aspects of him, hence the confusion. It follows that much of this book is about my version of 'knowing' Robert Lenkiewicz and is, therefore, to be seen as just one example of many different perceptions of the man.

In St Saviours – Robert's philosophy library.

At Robert's house in Plymouth.

I should mention that my style of contact with Robert was not a particularly unique arrangement. A similar link existed between Robert and Dr Philip Stokes, for example, dating back to the seventies. Sadly, though, Philip died before completing his larger work on Robert. However, some of his photographs are to be found in the book *R.O. Lenkiewicz* which is, effectively, Robert's autobiography presented in the form of an extended interview.

Lord St Germans and Michael Palmer were two other particular friends of Robert. They both had an extended relationship with him that undoubtedly had a confiding element. I am delighted that each felt able to contribute a piece for this book that catches their memories on his character, lifestyle and work, so broadening the account. I am most grateful that some of Robert's female friends also felt able to talk to me in depth and offer a description of Robert Lenkiewicz through the eyes and experiences of women closely involved with him. Their usual preference was to offer this contribution anonymously. Similarly, it has been of great value to meet and talk with John Lenkiewicz who, as Robert's brother, was able to give some important views on early family influences.

The book falls loosely into three sections. The first of these, 'Robert Lenkiewicz as a Presence', gathers together material from multiple sources and combines it with personal impressions from my various meetings with him, and also from studying some of his written work. This section muses on the complex and unusual personality behind an almost unique lifestyle and an abnormally prolific creativity.

A second section takes the theme, 'Lenkiewicz as a Painter'. Readers should not look for expert commentary from myself on Robert's paintings per se, although there are a good number of images of his paintings included. However, the gap is filled by invited comments and a mix of quotations from a range of people who have had contact with Robert's work. Included here is an informative contribution by Louise Courtnell who writes from the perspective of a pupil of Robert's, and also as a current figurative painter.

The final section, 'Towards an Understanding', takes on a somewhat more psychological bias exploring a little of the family background and resultant psychodynamics that gave Robert his exceptional drive and promoted the recurring themes in some of his paintings. I attempt an explanation of his proneness to sexual profligacy and examine the psychosomatic factors that may well have played a part in his premature death.

Simon Butler, the arts publisher, best catches the spirit of this book when he writes, 'the more complex the artist the more we need to know about his life in order to 'appreciate' his work.' This then is an effort at setting the products of Lenkiewicz the painter into some sort of context by adding glimpses of his recent life and his approach to life as seen through the eyes of a clinical psychologist and some of his other friends. I should emphasise that this is not an art book as such and I do not follow the conventions of such books. Also, my approach to photography is not that of the professional. It was more a case of 'opportunist snaps', some of which became the foundation for this memorial to Robert.

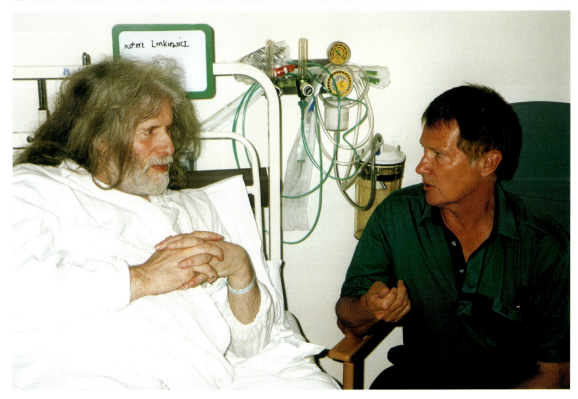

Discussions in Derriford Hospital.

Robert LENKIEWICZ AS A PRESENCE

LENKIEWICZ AS A CIVIC PRESENCE

One of the fading murals in Plymouth.

Since Robert's death it has become very evident that people miss him and would like him back. Conversations today with people who dwelt close enough to see him regularly in the Barbican area of Plymouth, and also with those who were devotees of his painting or who supported and worked with him, are almost inevitably imbued with loss and regret. In part this is because he had a presence that was atypical and very powerful. It was also a reliable presence in the sense that he rarely left the region, worked seven days a week, never changed his basic appearance and manner of dress (other than ageing) and continued, with slight variations of theme, to do the same thing year after year.

Despite his earlier 'difficult years' when he tormented local authorities he had become a generally more valued figure during his last decade and had achieved a positive civic presence. This took a physical form through his exhibition room, studio and now faded murals in the Barbican. Added to this, as a continuing visual reminder of Lenkiewicz, most serious galleries in the Barbican locality would (and still do) display originals or prints of his work and, at times, some galleries featured occasional small-scale exhibitions on a Lenkiewicz theme. There have also been larger public exhibitions, the more notable being the retrospective that took place at the City of Plymouth Museum and Art Gallery in 1997. This achieved the status of a major civic event with various dignitaries present. Similarly, an event took place in March 2002 at the Plymouth Museum and Art Gallery at which the Mayor of Plymouth formally handed over the St Saviours Church building to provide a location for Robert's philosophy library.

Prior to this Robert had provided 'An Evening with Robert Lenkiewicz' at Plymouth Theatre Royal in 1996, and made 'royal' visits to various minor functions. He also provided short talks or lectures in the locality, an example being a lecture on Goya given at Plymouth's Art Centre. Regional newspapers sometimes reported the annual Christmas Day dinner that he provided at the bus station for homeless people. It is of note that Plymouth University thought it appropriate to award him an honorary PhD in 2001 in recognition of his stature as a painter.

Robert was a striking, tall figure with long greying hair and would be recognised by a great number of people in various locations and functions in the Plymouth area. Thus, latterly, Robert had indeed become an integral and well known part of the general cultural atmosphere of Plymouth.

The day after his death the regional newspaper, the *Western Morning News*, described Robert as a 'larger than life character'. It is a rather vague and ridiculous portrayal in a sense but it does catch the fact that Robert was widely known for unusual and disturbing traits and also as a rare, powerful, creative talent. Such public statements add weight to the claim that he had become a strongly felt presence in Plymouth and the wider South West of England. Further supporting evidence comes in the media attention following his death and the continuing interest in the fate of his paintings and estate. Double-page spreads in newspapers and extended features in periodicals such as *Devon Life* emphasise the point.

In the address to the audience gathered at the Plymouth Museum to witness the handing over of St Saviours church for Robert's use as a library for his philosophy collection, the then Mayor of Plymouth said, 'Love him or loath him, you can't ignore him'. The statement (meant in a kindly way) captured an aspect of his presence that sometimes provoked disfavour, namely, Robert was prone to occasional sensationalised public events that were often misinterpreted as the acts of an ill-disciplined, perhaps delinquent self-publicist. He was also widely known within the broader locality for what was perceived as startling sexual extravagance. This has provoked a diversity of feelings from deep envy to gross outrage. Similarly, Robert's near lifelong habit of relating to, harbouring, and at times exploiting, local vagrants and homeless alcoholics tended to polarize judgements about him. On making general inquiries I have encountered various reactions to this habit. These range between those who admired what was perceived to be Robert's deep, feeling concern for the disadvantaged and, at the opposite end of the dimension, those who have left me somewhat shocked by their

Robert was a familiar figure about town.

Robert receives a cake marking the handing over of St Saviours Church building by the Mayor of Plymouth.

persisting anger towards him. Recently, a still rather bitter and angry local trader went as far as to say to me that Robert used to be hated by the traders and residents in his earlier days because 'He was a filthy tramp. We got fed up with the nuisance that he and his tramps caused'. He further expressed great distaste towards the 'leeches that hung around him and made use of him'.

In a very unkind (I suggest rivalrous) obituary that appeared in *The Times*, the anonymous author commented, 'his gift for publicity outran his skills with the brush.' In contrast, a year later on national television, the art critic David Lee commented, 'I've always considered Robert Lenkiewicz to be one of the most interesting of contemporary figurative artists'.

From a different but relevant perspective, the businessmen of Plymouth had begun to see him in positive terms; good for business perhaps. Thus, on local television, just after his death, Tim Jones of the Devon and Cornwall Business Council expressed the view that, 'He has been quintessentially the most iconic figure that Plymouth had in the cultural world'. Of his paintings, 'They have been wonderfully evocative images'.

In short, Robert had a strong but confused presence in the South West of England. Ambivalence is the word that best describes the overall perception of the man by his community although, in general, his presence was taking on an increasingly positive bias that evoked a growing acceptance and recognition of his great value and a true sense of loss of potential with his death. Dave Goodwin, the creator of a Lenkiewicz website, catches the spirit of all this when he writes later in this book:

I have simply been caught in the shadow he has cast over the city for the past three decades… seeing Lenkiewicz's work hanging above what seemed like every mantelpiece in the city, witnessing the creation of his murals, hearing the gossip and rumour and reading the newspaper headlines was all part of growing up in Plymouth. Robert Lenkiewicz simply could not be avoided.

LENKIEWICZ AS A PERSONAL PRESENCE
Observations and Personal Experiences

First and foremost Robert Lenkiewicz was a painter. A compulsive painter, I am probably justified in saying. Rather like a comet he left a trail in the places he routinely visited or lived in, although in his case it was a permanent trail. The trail was the atmosphere and physical presence of extraordinary creativity and an offbeat collector's zeal. Shortly before his death I made a number of visits to a studio area in his newly acquired premises in Castle Dyke. It was noticeable that often there were maybe a dozen or so large black empty canvases leaning against the walls together with an equal number of paintings, all in progress. Most of these paintings were in their very early stages though, some little more than a crude tentative outline using diluted oils as a statement of the painting to come. I put it to Robert on one

First and foremost Robert was a compulsive painter.

of these visits that he had an addiction to large black canvases and an associated compulsion to begin a painting on each of these. I added that he was possessed of less of a compulsion to finish the paintings though. He reflected for a moment and with a quiet laugh agreed that this was probably a valid assessment.

If one had entered a building without knowing that it was a Lenkiewicz haunt or abode it would soon be very obvious that he did have a presence in the premises. His hallmark was that of incessant creative industry, with a muddle of palettes, brushes, tubes of oilpaint and a clutter of reading material, preparatory sketches and notes, that were linked to certain paintings. To these were often added irrelevant artefacts, since collecting was an allied if less-powerful compulsion. These assorted items would draw attention simply by their very curious range: wooden carvings, old manual printing presses, religious sculpture, a grand piano, skulls, ancient books, a Citroen Deux Chevaux (that was being held for a possible romantic moment), modern videos and even an exercise bicycle (a product of fantasised fitness I suspect), represent a small sample of the numerous items scattered through various studio areas. He was, then, a compulsive painter and a compulsive collector, the latter often driven by arbitrary whim.

The familiar clutter of a studio area in Robert's house.

Personally, I found Robert to be very different from anyone else that I have known and could not help being inspired by him in various ways. Perhaps the best means of conveying this experience is through some notes written in the year 2001. As well as the notes taken with each visit that I made to meet him, I sometimes drew up overview notes around a particular

An addiction to black canvases.

A figure emerging from a statement.

Collector's zeal – carvings.

Collector's zeal – Robert's bizarrely but brilliantly placed piano at the top of stairs in a newly acquired warehouse.

Collector's zeal – it even included a Citroen 2CV hidden away in the Castle Dyke studio.

Lenkiewicz issue. What emerged was basically an essay as a guide to myself, setting out recent observations, experiences and conclusions and clarifying my reactions to myself. I will begin this appraisal of Lenkiewicz as a presence in peoples' lives with just such a memoir written after renewed contact following a brief break in meetings. It is a rationalisation of my relationship with Robert and serves to 'set out my stall' for this book.

NOTES

It is a Tuesday in October 2001 and I am driving down to see Robert once more. I am aware that this is probably about my thirtieth visit. It is raining and rather miserable and I am in a thoughtful mood on this rather tedious journey. A question is in my mind. Why do I keep going down to Plymouth to visit this man? I will carry this question with me through the visit.

As always it was an interesting visit. In fact, it is some months since I have seen Robert, something which seemed to take him by surprise. Not that I have not tried to meet with him. I have spoken to Yana on the phone quite a few times during that period to try to arrange an appointment. What was happening I'm not sure but, for a while, she inferred that Robert had been ill and was not making appointments and then, later, she was saying that she could not get him to settle with his diary to make arrangements. This all seemed to surprise

Robert who thought we had met about two months ago. He inferred that Yana was overprotective and said I should be more insistent and phone him directly. No matter. To be honest, in some ways the gap has been helpful since it has allowed me to glimpse the scale of his industry and productivity over a few months. I can report that it is daunting. He never ceases to amaze me with his dynamism. He is relentless in the way he pushes things forward and drives himself, despite fatigue and obvious health burdens. The volume of his creative output eclipses that of any other person in my knowledge – and they are not struggling with the problems and limitations of a degree of heart failure. Set against this the only demand Robert has in life appears to be his commitments to various projects – everything else is done for him by a large crew of mainly female supporters, a very fine arrangement.

We met in the Tudor Rose tea rooms. As has often been the case, Robert seemed tired and listless for the first few minutes. He looked well enough in his face. In fact, as always, he had a good colour and presented the quality of skin at sixty that many women in their thirties yearn for (his hatred of sunny weather plays a part in this, I believe). As we eased into our conversation he gained energy and leaned forward to talk with vigour. He gave me an overview of progress with some of his recent projects, talked of an interview with an MP who wanted to consult him on the theme of fanaticism (with regard to Afghanistan) and spiralled off into an impromptu thesis concerning the concept of the devil through the ages. I am in no position to judge his stature as a historian of religious and fanatical ideas but I trust him and my sense is that he is indeed exceptionally well read in this area and is without doubt a true and powerful expert source.

In the Tudor Rose tea rooms.

Time flits by in these conversations. They are intensely interesting. In relation to my question, though, 'interesting' does not quite catch it. I suppose a word that hovers in my mind is inspirational. In experiential terms I cannot find any descriptor which better catches it. There is something inspiring about his energy, creative momentum and sharp sense of direction in life.

Is this then why I stay motivated to visit him? Yes, in part, but there are other issues. At a basic level I like him and I think that he likes me. In general terms we are friends. But this is more a description than an answer. I am looking for explanation, not just description.

Something that I had been aware of for some years is that Robert has an unusual interpersonal 'gravitational' power. There exists a core of people around him

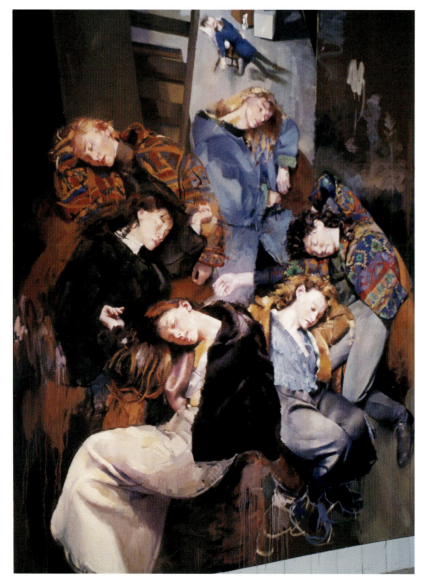

The Seven Sleepers of Ephesus (one of the many pictorial statements by Robert, unconscious perhaps, of his captivating power).

who, by analogy, are held in close orbit by this gravitational attraction. They support him, harbour him and make possible his remarkable productivity. This inner core, mainly women, are effectively devoting their lives to him. At one level they are trapped by his extraordinary interpersonal gravity. I can sense this pulling power too. It does have the effect of pulling one in closer as a devotee – rather (to use a crass Hollywood analogy) like a tractor beam from Starship Enterprise. But I don't want to be caught in this beam. It would be too humiliating for me to let the attraction take hold and then find oneself becoming a sort of supplicant, feeding on bits of attention. So I have developed a habit of remaining in distant orbit with visits from time to time. But, I have to confess, I do feel the pull of interpersonal gravity.

I should not drift into unconditional admiration though. There are, in general terms, some aspects of Robert's persona that could make one rather more circumspect. Some people hold a severely negative picture of him. I was at a function in Plymouth some years ago and ended up conversing with someone with a Social Services function. I mentioned my acquaintance with Robert adopting, it has to be said, a rather admiring stance and commenting that Plymouth was lucky to be Robert's host city. This provoked the angry response, 'That is not how I see him, in fact, I think he is a complete shit'. I did not inquire why he held this view or what situations provoked it but sensed, in principle, what he might be referring to. The truth of it is that I have seen nothing of the difficult side of Robert personally and so it is rather distant. Added to which, hopefully, I can deal with the issues in ways other than reflexive disapproval. Robert can appear disturbingly unfeeling at times in his dealings with people and I have no doubt that there are some wounded souls who feel abandoned along his path in life. Robert defends against seeing the damage he might do with a robust form of denial. 'Their attachment to me is just another form of addiction, it is physiological. It will hurt in withdrawal for a while but they will get over it.' (May 1998). Overall, though, I have not found him to be psychopathic in the exact sense of the term. He does have the capacity to be caring and sensitive, empathic even, but this capacity is often trampled underfoot by his extreme creative and (in the past) sexual energy that makes him drive himself ruthlessly forward, regardless of the cost to himself and others.

Why, as a psychologist, am I not judgemental about the potentially damaging side of Robert? This is where the answer to my question is located – this is why I keep journeying down to visit the man. In our conversations we sometimes achieve an interaction which is best described as deeply confiding. Through these exchanges I have come to know Robert as a curious and unusual mix of features but, above all else, he has a substance as a person which I deeply admire. Despite his inconvenient and possibly damaging ways, I think it is reasonable to say that currently there are enough, by far, of we pedestrian personalities and creative non-starters for the world to get by on but very few people of such compelling creative stature as Lenkiewicz. We should dwell with them gratefully, accepting as best we can their eccentricities and troubling impact. Robert's lifestyle is a hugely entertaining theatre that, at times, achieves a convincing simulation of the Renaissance ambience. As a historian of religious and supernatural ideation he is driven with a collector's zeal that has led to an assembly of literature, certain elements of which I have heard described by a senior academic as second only to the library at the British Museum. Having watched him paint and stood entranced by some of his paintings, his sheer skill as a figurative painter leaves me feeling that he might just as well be from another planet. He has also a rare skill in creating carefully judged environments which evoke great fascination. Here then is the answer. Robert, in my perception, has greatness, while, frankly, no one else that I know does.

Would I say that he is a great man? I am not sure of the difference. It is toying with words and drifting into excesses maybe. I'll stay reserved. I visit Robert Lenkiewicz because, unlike anyone else I know, he has a drive and creative capability that achieves, in my judgement, unambiguous greatness. That will do for now, it answers my question. That explains why I keep journeying down to Plymouth to visit him. I admire his greatness and enjoy seeing his products and being in the atmosphere that he creates.

It is not unqualified admiration, though, because I have to say 'beware the tractor beam and the damage potential therein' – a warning that comes too late for many of those who fell into close Lenkiewiczian orbit and became casualties.

Having finished our coffee at the Tudor Rose we adjourned to the Castle Dyke studio. Robert laboured up the hill, a tall, upright, apparently strong man but needing to walk slowly and pause occasionally as breathlessness from fading cardiac power gained hold. He showed me through the various rooms of the building again, each a separate studio. Eventually we came to my favourite area

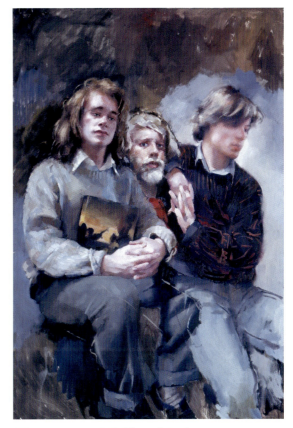

The painter with Wolfe and Reuben.

Robert's greatness as a painter — work well-advanced on The Last Supper, *October 2001.*

where I could do little other than stand absorbed, yet again, in front of Robert's painting of The Last Supper – it is a superb painting, this really is greatness. He truly does create such an intriguing atmosphere of greatness.

FIRST CONTACT AND SUBSEQUENT MEETINGS

My first exposure to the work of Lenkiewicz was at a local art exhibition in the Fairlynch Museum in Budleigh Salterton. It will have been about 1988, I believe. Maybe a hundred paintings were on display in a modest hall. It was the usual sort of thing for local art groups – boats in a harbour at low tide, nice country scenes and so on. But for me there was only one painting in the hall, it eclipsed everything. A large black canvas with a Rembrandt-like self portrait illuminated, in a style reminiscent of Caravaggio, by an invisible sidelight. It depicted a man with long hair and an imposing face seeming as if about to speak to an audience. It was not just a striking portrait with exquisite detail but it had a voice of subtle mystery that was curiously compelling. I went back to it again and again, entertained by the discovery that someone alive could and would paint in this style, and that the painter was an artist who worked in Plymouth.

Nothing else transpired from this visit. With the distractions of life, the presence of the name Lenkiewicz and the associated flurry of excitement attached to it receded from daily awareness. I foresaw no further outcome. However, in the summer of 1996 while on a cruise to Falmouth by yacht, poor weather led to my wife and I staying for three days or so in Plymouth's Sutton Harbour Marina. Inevitably, I suppose, we soon walked around the old quay area nearby, known as the Barbican. This proved a fateful move for, within five minutes walk, unexpectedly there before me was a small exhibition room with the title R.O. Lenkiewicz – Painter above its front window.

The title triggered the memory of the painting at Budleigh. The small exhibition area offered a collection of paintings dealing with vagrancy. Whilst clearly fine paintings, their theme was painful to me in some respects and they did not appeal in the immediate sense that I had expected. Intriguingly, though, there was a small sign inviting viewers to look in at the painter's studio four doors along on the right. The wooden door was located. It allowed entrance into a generally very creaky, old, rambling building that had clearly been a warehouse. Ascending a narrow staircase, I suddenly found myself in a huge, open, timber-roofed area that evoked what is best described as a 'psychological intake of breath'. The area was strewn with hundreds of paintings, it seemed. On the walls, stacked six to ten deep against the walls, on easels, some secured up in ceiling areas and others littered around smaller side studios – that included one with an ornate bed – paintings just everywhere. The lighting was well thought out and effective so creating a general visual array that was extremely successful in achieving great power and impact. Most of the paintings were portraits, many with multiple figures. In the side studios the volume of paintings was, if

One of many self portraits.

The studio in the Barbican, with Robert's fading mural to the right.

First impressions of the Barbican studio: the overwhelming pressure of creative talent.

The street scene entitled The Temptation of St Antony.

anything, greater. The impression of overwhelming productivity was intense. Breathtaking is not a word to use lightly but it applied at that moment. Later I learned of the general claim that Robert had produced over 10 000 paintings. It seemed feasible.

Probably the most dominant feature in the main area was an enormous painting, about forty feet in length and fifteen feet high, which was an apparent street scene with multiple figures that I later learned was called 'The Temptation of St Antony'.

In common with many, I found the initial impact of being in this 'chamber' rather startling. The profusion of work, the apparent skill of the figurative painter, the empathic depth in the depiction of facial expression, an undoubted element of sexual shock in some of the paintings, and just the sheer pressure of creative talent was remarkable. It overshadowed any artistic experience that I had encountered previously in life and evoked an immediate sense of a need to cling on to something that was very important here. The impact of the style of painting and, indeed, the general atmosphere of this huge studio appealed intensely at a personal level. It appealed to my own psychology quite perfectly. There was more though: the studio invited consideration professionally since, as is expanded later, the indications were of a man who combined a rare creative talent with an extremely driven, highly productive personality. Such features were of special interest to me in relation to a theory by the psychoanalyst, Elliott Jaques. He predicted that psychological changes in the mid life of highly creative painters would result in changes in their actual style of painting and, possibly, their premature death.

Fortuitously, Jane, Robert's personal assistant in the studio at that time, was working in the main section of the studio. She was a pretty woman with black hair and dressed exclusively in black with an impressive long black skirt combined with black boots. (Later I discovered that

Detail from St Antony.

this tended to be an informal dress code that Robert's female assistants tended to observe).

On impulse I asked Jane if Robert ever gave interviews. She inquired about the purpose and I confided that I was a clinical psychologist by profession and that aspects of Robert's work interested me and I would like to discuss them with him. Unexpectedly she said that this was perfectly possible and, picking up a huge vellum appointment diary, offered me a one-hour interview slot some weeks later.

Most people who have had personal contact with Robert remember the initial contact. Sally Moore describes later in this book how her legs went weak at the first sight of Robert. So, too, my first hour with Robert is a powerful memory, although not including weak legs I should add. I had been upstairs in the Barbican studio wandering around the hundreds of paintings, awaiting my appointment. Jane called to me and showed me downstairs to Robert's library. He was waiting at the foot of the stairs and immediately showed me into a most 'atmospheric' room. It was my first experience of Robert's second greatest talent – that of ever ongoing theatre. He was a master at exploiting carefully selected and cultivated props to create a Renaissance look-alike world. In keeping, then, he eased shut the hugely thick, heavy, ornate door whose hinges rasped dryly with an incredible creaking sound. He kept these hinges dry for deliberate effect, I later discovered.

We were in a tastefully lit room, quite small with a side annexe. It was crammed with the rich colours of many hundreds of books, a large old desk, a matching ornate chair for Robert and a lowly, functional piece for his visitors. In fact, Robert seemed very consistent with this particular trait. Wherever I met him he would immediately site himself in the best and sometimes only chair leaving the visitor to make do by perching on whatever might be to hand.

Robert presented in a manner that he never changed in all our contacts (except when in hospital). A tall, upright man of biggish build with shoulder-length and still-thick, once-brown hair now running to grey. A black painter's smock that clearly had a long history of paint daubs to honour its vintage dominated his dress. Under this were soft black leggings and, inevitably, as I learned, heavy brown boots. His face was strong but finely featured and, as noted earlier, remarkable for the quality of skin. Although fifty-five at the time, his skin was more like that of a thirty-year-old female model. He spoke in a quiet, cultured voice with a southern English pronunciation. Extracts from my notes at that meeting record the following encounter.

NOTES

An overview prepared from notes taken at the first meeting with Robert Lenkiewicz on Tuesday 19 November 1996

Having exchanged pleasantries Robert enquired my reason for requesting a meeting with him. I told him that, as a clinical psychologist, I was preoccupied with the span of his creativity and the sheer power of his productivity. Explaining that I had a special interest in health changes brought about by psychological traits I then launched into a brief review of an investigation by psychoanalyst Elliott Jaques. This explored the causes of loss of creativity and changes in creative style to a more reflective, slower output that, Jaques's research reveals, have occurred in the later years of various exceptionally creative people in the past*.

Robert watched me throughout what must have been a five minute exposition, listening intently with apparent great interest but without comment. I asked him for his view and whether he felt that his own creative style had changed and whether his productivity had faltered at all. He thought not. If anything he believed creative energy and productivity to be accelerating. He presented his work in general as a lifelong quest explaining that he regarded himself primarily as a communicator with painting skills. His task was that of making comment on sociological issues and human behaviour (especially fanaticism) while exploring his own theory of aesthetic attraction. I wrote down a literal transcript here – 'Aesthetic attraction in relationships, including the sexual element, is simply a form of physiological addiction. As such, interpersonal relationships do not merit, in my view, the status given in present society. Relationships between men and women are best seen as transitory and interchangeable.' Robert emphasised that he was totally opposed to the notion of lifelong marriage and contractual relationships. It then emerged that Robert organised his paintings in themes or projects in order to make such comment. There were twenty such 'projects'. Currently he was very busily engaged in Project 20 concerning addiction and addictive behaviour. This was to comprise 600 paintings. We talked around the theme of psychological state and its impact on physiological process for a while, touching on the basis of addiction.

First contact with Robert in his studio and library.

An unchanging dress habit.

* Because of its relevance, the theory of Elliott Jaques is outlined in the later section 'Towards an Understanding'.

Self Portrait with Self Portrait at Ninety.

Since I was not as well briefed as I might have been for the meeting, the 'sociological/communicator' emphasis came as something of a surprise. We discussed that through for a time, and then I moved things on to his painting per se. Here it all became a little confusing. I mentioned having looked at and been most impressed by his painting, Self Portrait with Self Portrait at Ninety. Reasonably, I thought, I asked him the meaning to be taken from the painting. Curiously and rather sharply he said, 'I am not a narrative painter, it's just a pun. It is Leonardo's body leaning against me and I have acquired Rembrandt's hand. The older figure holds the spiral helix of time. It's a pun.' I was disappointed and pressed him a little more over meaning and his paintings in general. Again, Robert would not have it. His paintings were 'primarily exercises in light, tone and depth.' It felt like great avenues of interesting exploratory conversation had just been closed off and I jotted rather irritably in my notes — 'the great communicator won't communicate'.

As the hour drew to a close I asked about Robert's place in the contemporary art scene. Unexpectedly, he responded rather bitterly saying, 'I am dismissed.' He then made reference to some prominent figures in the London art community whose approval he would welcome yet, generally, they held disparaging views about his contribution as a figurative painter. It seemed to trouble him but only in the sense of being reminded of an aggravation.

It was time to leave but as I stood up Robert said, 'I wonder if you would be prepared to sit for me?' I misunderstood what he was saying and so sat down again. Then it came to light that he wanted me to be a sitter for one of the paintings in his addiction project. Naturally, being flattered, I agreed but asked why? He said it was because he thought I truly understood the perspective he held concerning the addictive physiology of aesthetic taste. In all honesty I did not think that I had understood it since it all seemed a bit vacuous to a clinical psychologist imbued with a need for objectivity and supporting evidence. But I was not going to tell him that. It was agreed, though, I would come back in two weeks for a first sitting.

Robert wanted to show me around his library and its annexe for five minutes before leaving. I soon grasped that there was another aspect to Lenkiewicz. He was a rather obsessed collector of ancient texts and materials on witchcraft, philosophy, theology and religious ideation. Fanaticism seemed to have a predominant place in his interests. He pointed out various (apparently) extremely important old manuscripts that were recent acquisitions that he seemed truly excited about.

Later, sitting with a coffee at a café in the Barbican, I was again left slightly agitated by a feeling of having been in contact with something that I had to cling on to because it was rare and valuable. It was Robert, in fact, who was rare and valuable. An eccentric who had created a physical environment of great artistic and intellectual richness. It was a troubling feeling but it was reassuring to have an arrangement to return for my first experience as a sitter within two weeks.

Robert AS A MAN A PORTRAIT IN WORDS

It would be presumptuous to present what appears to be a definitive statement on precisely how Lenkiewicz was as a person. There need to be at least a dozen such statements simply because he presented different aspects of himself to differing sets of people. The general consensus is that during the last two decades no one person enjoyed the true, complete Lenkiewicz.

Robert's relationship with women was clearly very different in comparison to that established with male friends, especially those men who had become regular contacts. Many of these appear to have been treated as confidants to one degree or another. In fact the relationship held with male friends seems to have been rather more consistent than that with women, although different male friends had different functions for Robert, some practical and functional, others more intellectual. In contrast, there appeared to be much more variance in the character of his relationships with women. A large circle of women sitters who visited him with varying frequency appeared to enjoy a sincere, often sexual, but relatively superficial relationship with Robert. In distinction, there were a small number of women who had very frequent contact with him and a fairly full knowledge of many of his activities. This is because he treated them as trusted confidants too.

There was also, as Robert himself portrayed it, a further small circle of 'key' women in his life towards whom, paradoxically, he related with a growing tendency towards secretiveness. This was curious in the sense that he was, in the main, affectionate and grateful to them because he depended on them. Yet, despite recognising his dependence on them, he also indicated quite clearly that he saw them as a threat to his freedom to continue expanding his book collection and pursue the necessary deals to service the consequent burgeoning debt. He needed freedom from constraint and complaint in order to risk even greater debt through the acquisition of further premises for his future galleries and studios.

Robert also made clear that he felt it most important to guard his freedom to continue 'work' on the 'aesthetic notes' (sexual diaries). The latter were large books of notes illustrated with drawings and watercolours that were kept as a record of the physical and emotional experiences of various sexual partners during sexual encounters. He persisted to the end of his working life with these diaries. Secretiveness was therefore very much part of the atmosphere that I ran into right from the beginning of our contact. From his point of view it was essential, although it has to be said that there was an immature element of boyish delight in what he thought was his talent for 'getting away with it' that tended to feed this secretive habit.

All this reduces down to the fact that his relationships were encapsulated one from another, and each of us knew differing aspects of Robert. Fortunately, some of Robert's male and female friends have spoken with me very openly concerning their experiences with him and the presence that he had in their lives. This has helped greatly in building up a picture of the ways in which he operated with different types of people. Disappointingly, some of the women he was close to during the last ten years or so have felt unable to write about or even describe to me Robert as a presence in their lives. Some declined, arguing that their relationship was so intensely private and that it was unsuitable for discussion. Another lacked the freedom because of ongoing legal process. Fortunately, though, some women did not feel quite so constrained and have helped considerably in building a wider picture through anonymous contributions. Even so, what follows must be seen as a picture based primarily on my own contact, observations and conversations with Robert. Inevitably some will say, 'he was not like that' – it has happened already. In this case my reply has to be, 'this is how he was with me.'

The 'Statement' for Michael Foot, centre painting.

As will be described later, when Robert began a portrait he would initially use turpentine-diluted paint to 'draft' out the outline of the painting to be on the selected canvas. This he referred to as the 'Statement' of the painting. In describing him in more detail as a person it is fitting to imitate this approach of his in verbal form. So I will begin with a set of brief, bold statements that make up the elements of my statement of a verbal portrait of Robert Lenkiewicz. Then I will add in some more detail:

Multiple 'Statements'.

The Author's 'Statement' OF HIS PORTRAIT OF ROBERT

An atmospheric, theatrical presence combined with an intensity and quiet charm • A showman by instinct • A personal appeal that evoked in others feelings of intense possessive loyalty and a need to be regarded by him as special • Relating to key helpers as if they were parents or wardens to be circumvented • Deeply intellectual with a powerful knowledge base • A relentless creative momentum • Meticulous scheduling and time management • Secretive but unable to keep his own secrets • Continual intrigue with endless scheming and dealing • Not well travelled and not well schooled in the skills of the contemporary world • Creating the clutter, interest and obsession of a collector • Out of control in relation to his addiction for rare, ancient books • Capable of being social and homely • Curious humour • Boyish enthusiasms • Prone to outrageous actions • Unexpected loyalties, a preoccupation with the dispossessed • Prone to denial of health risks yet a theatrical invalid • An intense interest in women with extravagant sexual excess • Transient interest only in individual women yet unable to take responsibility to end a relationship • Charitable, generous but capable of temper and harshness • Apparent modesty yet a very strong sense of purpose and a very strong self image – he knew he was different, remarkable and important.

THE LENKIEWICZ ATMOSPHERE

I have met very few people who did not find Robert both captivating and fascinating. A few could 'take him or leave him', a few have resented him or been frightened of him because they have encountered claims that he was a sexual predator, and a few have been extremely cross with him. To be with him was a distinctly different experience from that of conventional encounters. He had a very cultured manner combined with a sense of intensity and, it has to be said, importance. Face to face he could be a good listener if required but was more inclined to be a good talker. He was well aware of his superiority in terms of capability in and knowledge of art, and also the superiority of his reading in aspects of philosophy and theology. He gave the impression that it felt normal to him to be listened to as an informed expert. It clearly felt normal to him that a psychologist should regularly reappear and take an interest in him because he knew he was distinctive, different and interesting. In the extended interview that led to the book *R.O. Lenkiewicz*, Robert states (concerning his youth), 'I had a very powerful, immature sense of destiny: no doubt about it'. I do not believe that this sense of destiny ever left him. In fact, a small aid in assessing Robert's sense of difference and importance is to be found in the very existence of the various versions of his biography, long and short, that were produced by the time he was in his mid fifties.

Because Robert was so focused on his paintings, projects, deals and collecting there was a constant stream of change and development in his life. It meant that each visit I made was rather like a 'soap' on television. Like others, I found myself keen to catch up with the next events in the fast moving plot, especially since his health was fading and there was the added drama of time running out, yet a dramatic sense that somehow he would battle through by effort of will and survive. He carried the atmosphere of the pre-eminent and key player in an unfolding drama. Naturally people would turn to look at him. Naturally they would want a bit of his time and attention, naturally they would want to be noticed by him. My point is that he did have atmosphere – an aura even.

THEATRICAL TALENTS

This atmosphere was prone to become theatrical though, sometimes on a grandiose scale and sometimes in little, almost unassuming ways. I developed an affection for these little bits of theatre. For example, in his last two years we would often meet during a lunch time at his Basement studio. It was not practical to stay in the main painting area itself because it was a tiny room and hopelessly crowded with paintings and easels. Accordingly, we would settle for the equally tiny rear secondary studio (that also doubled up as a bedroom) as a venue for lunch. Having edged past paintings and general clutter, Robert would settle in the only chair and immediately become an invalid, placing a pillow or blanket across his legs in theatrical triumph, I rather thought. It is true that, at the time, his health was fading but he was not ill

The 'invalid' in the Basement studio.

as such and had been functioning with normal vigour prior to that moment. Meantime, I would perch incongruously and uncomfortably on the edge of the bed, peripherally aware that it was the 'work centre' for much of the content of the ongoing sexual notes project. Similarly, on visiting his house on one occasion, I found him working, again with normal vigour, but as soon as he had set this aside and stopped to talk he retreated to his couch. There, he wrapped himself in a blanket for half an hour, role playing, it seemed, the wise elder with (to use a term that he enjoyed) an ague.

This love of theatricality was well recognised locally. Speaking to a gallery owner in the Barbican some years ago he said to me:

NOTES
6 September 1999

'He is a terrific painter but it's the pure theatre of it all that I love best. It is all calculated, of course, the dark interiors, the atmosphere of the medieval. Great theatre, terrific stuff. The artist's psychoses are half the attraction'

Visits to Robert's cottage in Plymouth allowed one little tastes of his sense of a theatrical environment. Robert was fully aware the cottage was itself an 'exhibition piece' because he had clearly so designed it. He also clearly enjoyed exhibiting it. On 20 May 1998, in the middle of general conversation about the addiction project he suddenly said 'Have you seen my cottage? I would like you to make a visit. Bring your camera.'

The shady approach to Robert's front door.

A few weeks later I made my first visit there, discovering Robert's cottage to be a distinctive enclave of thoughtful difference in an otherwise plain suburbia. After various visits my impression was that Robert had used his cottage as a means of creating another environment as an exhibit. He was proud of it and encouraged me to roam freely with my camera.

In the same sense that the rambling Barbican studio had a 'three centuries ago' time-warp feel about it, so too did his cottage. One entered the walled garden through a gate that inevitably swung on dry, distressed hinges, walking up through a rather pleasant, shady, natural garden towards a front door. The wall just to the left of the door boasted ten or more gravestones leaning carelessly against it as adornments. An exterior table near the front door used a large gravestone as the table top. It was a long cottage with rather minimal concessions to heating, and relatively small windows that often had shutters closed to keep out sunlight. Bare stone walls, furnishings and the general décor all gave the desired, timeless, 'this house does not belong in modern Plymouth nor in this century' feel about it. Assertions of Robert's affinity with the beloved Renaissance era were carefully constructed to good effect. The only blot on the scene was a somewhat out of place television and some modern table lights. The kitchen area was also a contrived antique, rather 1920s was my impression,

Gravestones lean beside the front door.

The exhibit – Robert's 'not in this century' cottage décor.

and rightly so, too, for contemporary kitchen designers would have no place in such an environment.

In a later refurbishment of the western end of the cottage Robert became more expansively and expensively theatrical, I felt. It was beautifully done with some lovely woodwork. He was most proud of a very tall door that he had commissioned based on the design of a door in a Saxon church that he loved – 'You must take a photo of my Saxon door'. I did not ask what it cost but it would not have been cheap. A wonderfully handsome antique log-burning stove also took on trophy status in the living room during this time, a further emblem of his restless acquisitiveness.

CURIOUS HUMOUR

Sometimes public events served as a focus for various of Robert's theatrical talents on a more grandiose scale. The opening of the Retrospective Exhibition at Plymouth Museum in 1997 saw a fine combination of his delight in creating theatrical happenings, his curious humour and his complex, enduring relationship with vagrant and dispossessed people:

The door in the style of a Saxon church.

A further acquisition.

NOTES

9 August 1997

I have travelled to Plymouth Museum to see Robert's new exhibition – his Retrospective. There has been a growing excitement in the air about this for several weeks. My sittings and discussion sessions with Robert have often been interrupted by phone calls regarding the organisation of the event and the reception to follow it. Robert seems to regard it as his biggest event in Plymouth to date – something of a watershed in terms of local recognition.

As I arrived at the museum a sizeable crowd, including Robert and various of his 'ladies', stood gathered outside the entrance to the museum. We stood barred from entry by closed doors, regaled by a large banner stating 'R.O. Lenkiewicz – Retrospective'. The crowd boasted some dignitaries including Terry Waite (who was later to open the exhibition by making a speech. A red carpet led up to the museum doors creating a sense of high expectation. We were all encouraged by the implications of the red carpet – it promised that someone or something of significant import was surely headed our way. After a patient wait on the part of the dignitaries and we of the crowd a black limousine drew up. A uniformed chauffeur stepped around the vehicle to open the rear door and help out (to general surprise) the diminutive, for once well dressed, somewhat sheepish looking figure of Les Ryder, one of Robert's long standing vagrant sitters.

The joke was on the dignitaries and the rest of us. Robert [who up to the moment of arrival had been standing nearby] beamed with pleasure as Les walked the red carpet into the museum, whose doors solemnly swung open for him, while we all clapped him in. This was a classic moment of highly-organised, double-edged, Lenkiewiczian humour. Enormously theatrical and, at one level, childish and somewhat insulting to figures of stature. At another level (to make an interpretation), it was a compassionate affirmation of his value for the dispossessed and a reminder to us all, through the momentary inversion of social standings, that there is an inherent and punitive blindness to human value imposed by the social hierarchy that we all, unthinkingly, give service to in our rather snobbish society. Added to this, in tribute to Robert's fairness, Les *was* a kind of meritorious dignitary in the sense that he was a regular sitter and some of Robert's better portraits feature him. That being said, we all quickly poured in behind Les, soon forgetting Robert's poignant moment of kindly rebuke, thence to engage in the heady middle class activity of listening to a speech, followed by viewing and evaluating the painter's work. Les disappeared (or was disappeared) as the dignitaries took over and we art lovers swarmed around the exhibition in ardent conversation.

The moment arrives.

A crowd in anticipation.

Les Ryder being clapped in by a beaming Robert.

Les Ryder was a 'sitter' dignitary.

Art lovers' delights take over.

Although a deeply thoughtful man Robert had another, more conventional side to his humour. Sometimes he would lapse into story-telling, lampooning people and events in his life. Other times he would present a cherished joke that he had recently encountered with no inhibitions whatsoever in the mode of telling, nor concerning the content. Jewish jokes, sexual jokes, 'whatever was going around the street' jokes, they all appealed. Added to which, as I observed and as many of his close circle also confirmed to me, he loved the opportunity for a performance and embellished his stories and jokes with quite passable imitations and accents.

Robert was prepared to put extraordinary effort into elements of his humour, labouring with almost bizarre intensity to produce a personal, practical joke. On one visit to his house I spotted what appeared to be some old, one suspected priceless, illuminated pages from a medieval manuscript left spoiling in bright sunlight by a window. Asking why he was risking them to ultra violet he said that he had recently acquired some very old blank parchment and had reproduced illustrations from some pages of a genuine manuscript on this parchment. He was now deliberately ageing them in sunlight. The point was that a friend of his claimed always to be able to judge if old manuscripts were genuine or not. Robert, though, believed he could reproduce the illustrator's style exactly and age the illustrations artificially and so planned to fool his friend. This little humorous challenge will have taken hours to execute.

Robert, like the rest of us, had various modes of conversational style. Lord St Germans recalls that in the presence of guests taking dinner at Port Eliot he would sometimes adopt the manner of a professor relating to pupils, 'Blinding guests with a dazzling knowledge of the history of art, the whole thing peppered with quotes from memory.' Others have suggested that, despite his breadth of reading, Robert did have insecurities concerning his educational background (Secondary Modern schooling) and sometimes clearly ducked actual challenging debate by sheltering behind a smokescreen of quotation and historical knowledge. I never witnessed this personally but he certainly could get into an expansive flow when on a one to one basis but never, in my experience, gratuitously. An inviting question, for example, 'What was the general attitude to witchcraft in the sixteenth and seventeenth century?' could easily evoke a ten minute, uninterrupted exposition from Robert. I found him capricious in this behaviour though. Often, when I really wanted something of length from him, he would be disappointingly brief and non-committal, especially in relation to any analysis of his own paintings. This takes us to the issue of Robert as an intellect.

Fake illuminated pages being deliberately aged.

ROBERT LENKIEWICZ AS AN INTELLECT

He had, by most accounts, an unusually wide and strong grounding (self taught to a large extent it seems) in classical philosophy, with a very impressive recall and apparent ability to state the main elements of various philosophers' systems and statements. The biographical accounts that he gave to me follow those given elsewhere. He recounted that at the age of seventeen he met a Hungarian philosopher, one Alfred Rheinhold, who had formed a local philosophical society. This had appealed to Robert and he soon earned a niche for himself in the society by offering pen and ink drawings of classical philosophers such as Nietzsche, Goethe, Schweitzer, Socrates etc. for the society's magazine. Robert's involvement stemmed from a growing interest in philosophy in part acquired through a casual reading of encyclopaedias and discussion with certain residents at his parents' hotel. Apparently, Rheinhold took on a tutorial function with Robert and had some influence on the development of his philosophical reading and enlightenment.

In conversation with me Robert would, on occasions, make remarks that betrayed his prevailing reference to the issues, thinking and solutions of the earlier philosophers. Similarly, in his preparatory notes for the projects, significant paintings or just watercolour sketches linked to some thought of the day, the intellectual allegiance to loved philosophers would surface from time to time. Nietzsche seemed to hold a prominent place in Robert's thoughts to the extent that Robert phoned me in some excitement late one night in August 1999 to announce that three programmes were to be screened on television dealing with Nietzsche, Heidegger and Sartre, starting with Nietzsche even later that night. I can admit with shame that I relied upon the video recorder.

An interesting watercolour with accompanying notes catches the preoccupations and intellectual exercises that Robert undertook. He had clearly been reading and agonising on the theme of tragedy using W. J. Dannhauser's, *Nietzsche's View of Society*, 1974, and, as his notes infer, drawing on W. Kaufmann's *Nietzsche and the Death of Tragedy*, 1976. Examples of Robert's handwritten notes, which are to be seen framing the sketch in one of his notebooks, are set out below and can be made out in the photograph of the illustration. These notes are of interest not because Robert was the author of many of them but because they meant so much to him that he reproduced the mix of exact quotations alongside his illustrations. They tell us where his thoughts were at the time and what mattered to him. They are also of interest as an 'everyday' indication of the intellectual depth that Robert would work at.

In the absence of a title, I have labelled the item 'Illustration and notes – Rothko's Suicide'. At top right an introductory question sets the theme of the illustration. It concerns the death of the American expressionist painter Mark Rothko. Rothko suffered repeated episodes of depression and committed suicide in 1970. The question:

> *'Rothko? Could Derrida and Wittgenstein have stopped you committing suicide?'*

Robert then responds with a quotation (presumably from Kaufmann):

> *In one sense the Dionysian-Appoline dialectic represents an answer – and a quite original answer – to a question which had occurred to Plato and which clearly concerns Aristotle: why do we get pleasure from tragedy? ...Aristotle's formula that 'tragedy produces the pleasure that springs from pity and fear'. Nietzsches' answer is coherent and impressive. Tragedy presents us with the destruction of individuals in a way which is exciting, because it gives us a glimpse of the underlying deeper power of life, in which we have a share, but which is only glimpsed when individuality is transcended.*

Illustration and notes – Rothko's Suicide.

Robert then adds a comment of his own:

> *And so it goes on, this stuff of Art, this anarchic intuitive rambling, precipitous and flowing, edgy then absent. Rothko? Could Derrida and Wittgenstein have stopped you committing suicide?*

The inquiry into tragedy is extended by a further quotation placed bottom left on the page:

> *Any realistic notion of tragic drama must start from the fact of catastrophe. Tragedies end badly. The tragic personage is broken by forces which can neither be fully understood nor overcome by rational prudence. This again is crucial where the causes of disaster are temporal, where the conflict can be resolved by technical or social means, we may have*

serious drama but not tragedy. More pliant divorce laws could not alter the fate of Agamemnon; social psychiatry is no answer to Oedipus. But saner economic relations or better plumbing can resolve some of the grave crises in the drama of Ibsen. The distinction should be borne sharply in mind. Tragedy is irreparable.

G. Steiner: The Death of Tragedy, *1961*

Finally, bottom right, an extract of points that seem to catch a fundamental value that Robert held:

To us art is an adventure into an unkown world which can be explored only by those willing to take risks. It is a widely accepted notion among painters that it does not matter what one paints as long as it is well painted. This is the essence of academicism. There is no such thing as good painting about nothing. We assert that the subject is crucial and only that subject matter is valid which is tragic and timeless.

This was 'early' Lenkiewicz and I have never discussed it with him, unfortunately. I would have put it to him that the anti-depressant powers of the work of Derrida and Wittgenstein are unlikely to have proved sufficient in the case of recurrent depression. Not the least reason being that the deconstructionist obscurity of Derrida would seem more likely to inflame depression rather than challenge it. It would have been a good debate. It is telling that both Nietzsche and Derrida appeal strongly to Lenkiewicz. We should note that both philosophers wrote to urge the abandonment and destruction of the accepted 'certainties' of their time, such as religion. Latterly, I have become increasingly aware of the heavy influence that philosophers like Nietzsche seem to have had on Robert's thinking, self image and lifestyle and discuss this aspect later in the book.

Casual pieces of this type are to be found in various of Robert's notebooks. He mused a great deal and found the time and physical energy to record his thoughts. His notes are littered with references drawn from his extensive reading, with quotes and reactions to that reading. The presentation is scholarly and the discussion logical and well informed.

In contrast, there were times in general conversation when I found that Robert could be less than clear. Brief excursions into his personal theories of aesthetic addiction as the basis of love and fanaticism did, on certain occasions, leave me thinking that he was being obscure. But I have to be mindful of the possibility that the deficit was mine, not his. Added to which, modern psychology tutors its graduates into the requirement that everything must be systematic, available for objective scrutiny and so, eventually, evidence based – as one would expect from a discipline that attempts to be a science. It can make the acceptance of different modes of thought more of a struggle and that is what I found at times with Robert's own theorising. My scientific bias was not always at peace with Robert's more lyrical, less constrained flow of thoughts and claims. Because of this I was inclined to 'ride along' with some of Robert's theory, especially that of aesthetic addiction. He referred to it regularly but did not develop it beyond the level of a general, rather loose claim. It was not presented in a scientific mode but on one occasion he did offer a private exposition which was relatively clear – as I recorded after one of my visits:

NOTES
Wednesday 2 July 1997
Lunch in the Basement studio

I took lunch in for Robert and he made me a revolting cup of tea in the grubby little kitchen area of the premises. We settled in the rear room, with myself perched on the corner of the bed as usual and he in his chair. After a ten minute 'knock about' session with a couple Jewish jokes from him and a story or two from me I edged towards the issue of his relationship with his children and their mothers.

In particular, I questioned him concerning the problem of the children and women becoming attached to him and their reaction to his non-availability for conventional and stable relationships. He dismissed the issue saying, 'Oh, it hurts for a while but they soon get over it, it is just a physiological addiction.' Then came a brief, spontaneous exposition of his theory of addictive reactions and aesthetic fascism. Using himself as both a constant observer of human behaviour and a 'guinea pig' involved in multiple relationships for research purposes he 'discovered' that love and jealousy involve intensely physical feelings in relation to the threat of and actual experience of losing a relationship. Loss of a relationship involves physical sensations very similar to that of physiological withdrawal in substance dependency. Thus, he argued, the intense, immediate feelings of attraction, attachment and love in relationships are actually an addiction event – physiologically based. Hence, aesthetic addiction. Addicted people become possessive of their 'fix', whether it be alcohol, cannabis or a specific person. Hence aesthetic fascism is born, that is, relating to others as if they were necessary property and acting out a lifelong dependency through the expectation of lifelong relationships. This leads into his (not original) notion that we project our own needs in our perception of significant others and thus the core of a relationship is less about the other and more about the self. Finally, Robert went on to say that he believed irrational, that is fanatical, responses to political and religious systems was an equivalent phenomenon of addictive reaction that left the exponent unavailable for change and prone to brutal and inhuman behaviour when there is threat to the adopted ideas.

Taking a risky line I pointed out to Robert an obvious paradox that, despite the inference that we should strive for addiction-free relating, his whole style of personal presentation seemed aimed at 'hooking' people into an addiction to Robert Lenkiewicz. He smiled, demurred briefly and then seemed to tire of the conversation.

A curiosity concerning Robert's all-pervasive theory of aesthetic addiction is that he regularly refers to physiology and physiological reaction. In reality, he had little education in the physiological field and, as far as I could tell, knew very little about physiology. In fact, in his main biography he states, 'What do I know about neurophysiology?' He used the word physiology as a label for a complex concept of his own, based on physical feelings that he had experienced. Then he extended this to try to account for certain phenomena in human relating and fanatical thought and behaviour. He basically agreed to the suggestion that he found aspects of fanatical thought and behaviour inexplicable and sought to account for these with reference to human functions other than rational thought. Similarly, he found great convenience in his theory and associated 'research' as a rationale for his totally disinhibited approach to sexual relations.

It was, though, in writing about the history of the development of religious, social and cultural concepts where I believe Robert achieved his best performance as a communicator. When preparing formal pieces Robert could write with great clarity and insight, demonstrating an impressive depth of learning and a skill in written communication. I would recommend that readers take a look at two pieces prepared by Robert that serve as excellent examples. Firstly, his 'Notes on The Last Judgement' (currently available as a reproduction by the Lenkiewicz Foundation, published in 2004). These notes are, in fact, a scholarly review of the history of the popular ideas and religious concepts of death, judgement, the afterlife and salvation through the Middle Ages and after. A brief extract earns the space as an example of Robert's writing:

> *The people of the early Middle Ages awaited the return of Christ without the fear of the Last Judgement…*
> *By the twelfth century, the apocalyptic scene, trumpeting angels, supernatural creatures, the gigantic Christ, arms outstretched leaks into Saint Mathew's imagery.*
> *Three basic features appear, the resurrection of the bodies of the just, the acts of judgement, the separation of the just who go to heaven, from the damned, who are plunged into eternal fire…*
> *One cannot help being struck by the almost clandestine manner in which hell and its torments have been introduced. It is not long before Mathew's edict: 'Depart from me, ye cursed, into ever lasting fire,' becomes fundamental.*
> *Not one of the people of God, let alone the unbeliever, is now assured of salvation. By the*

The monograph 'The Last Judgement'.

thirteenth century the concept of judgement was now dominant. Christ sits on the judge's throne...

The later Middle Ages saw human life as a long legal process: as a relationship between a personal biography and a judicial conception of the world. Each moment of life will be weighed some day in a solemn hearing... the creature responsible for this weighing is St Michael who becomes the patron saint of the dead.

How did the angelic examiner know about the acts that he had to evaluate? The answer is that they had been recorded in a book by another angel, half court clerk, half accountant.

The actions of the individual are no longer lost in the limitless space of transcendence, or the collective destiny of the species. From now on they are individualised. The new book-keeping spirit of businessmen, who were beginning to discover their own world – which has become our own – was applied to the content of life as well as to merchandise or money... By the eighteenth century, the big collective book of Revelation had become an individual booklet, a kind of passport or police record to be presented at the gates of eternity.

Robert Lenkiewicz

Secondly, as part of a curious personal exploration of blindness Robert decided to produce a series of paintings while totally blindfolded. These were all to be based on the 'Theme of Blind Tobit', a story concerning a pious Israelite and his son who journey with a disguised angel. As part of the venture Robert prepared a short monograph on blindness and culture – 'Paintings Painted Blind' *R.O. Lenkiewicz*, 2000. Once again he produces a delightful and informed little history of attitudes towards and understanding of blindness in different ages and cultures. As always, though, the emphasis in the content concerns thought during the Middle Ages and Renaissance eras – his span of interest and reading did not move on to the research and theory in perception of the twentieth century.

Many average painters just paint. The more intellectual, perhaps, paint to a theme or construct and are then able to give a rationale for the progression of their work. Thus saying, it would be negligent to finish with the issue of Robert as an intellect without comment on his set of twenty projects, each centred on a stated rationale such that, in this mode, he referred to himself as a communicator on sociological issues.

These projects are described at some length in the book *R.O. Lenkiewicz*. For a much briefer review of the concept underlying each project the booklet *R.O. Lenkiewicz: Brief Biography* (undated), that used to be on sale in the Barbican studio, is helpful. After a short self-characterisation and personal history all delivered in the third person he introduces notes on his projects with the sentence, 'His life in the city of Plymouth has consisted of a wide ranging and energetic series of thoughts and activities from which carefully-presented projects

The monograph 'Paintings Painted Blind'.

emerged.' In a subsequent *Guide to the Retrospective Exhibition* in 1997, opening once more with a short biography written in the third person, Robert expands the general rationale for the projects. Basically they are a mix of expressions of social concern and intellectual inquiry: 'Throughout this period he has been working intensively on the first of a long series of projects which he termed The Relationship Series' and *'He suggests in many notes that our understanding of the causes of fascism may be helped by enquiring into human behaviour in relation to falling in love, theological persuasions and belief systems.'* [Author's italics].

The twenty projects all exist and, according to the first of these guides, had a projected number of paintings totalling 6400. This somewhat startling figure excludes the landscape series. I am not clear on the extent to which projected numbers were actually achieved in the earlier years with his youthful rush of energy. For example, 'Vagrancy, 500 paintings, Mental Handicap, 500 paintings' and so on. Certainly, later projects such as Addiction with its projected 600 paintings had only reached about 150 paintings, with some of these not finished when he died.

In this endeavour to produce paintings to illustrate social issues and intellectual inquiries Robert's need to do things on a huge scale prevails. The numbers seem arbitrary but conceived to impress by sheer scale. This is also evident in his writing about the projects, in particular the *Guide to the Retrospective Exhibition*. It is worth the effort of first hand assessment and can still be obtained through the Lenkiewicz website and at auctions. My own reaction to this guide was one of mixed feelings. Robert writes to reveal a clearly expressed social concern, at the same time revealing a history of ineffectual 'angry young man showmanship' that probably alienated those he sometimes sought to influence in earlier years. Parts of the guide give evidence of great thoughtfulness, extensive reading and an inquiring intellect that impressed me. With other parts I found myself ill at ease because it felt more like he was indulging in a performance to impress rather than communicate, rather like a high-wire philosophical circus performer, seeking to dazzle readers with a bombardment of quotations and references. The product, for me, felt like a mixture of obscure, sometimes pompous and self-admiring material blended with glimpses of compassion, insight and deep inquiry that merit respect. Whatever else one says, though, this guide clearly confirms that Robert was deeply thoughtful and inquiring. His reading was extensive and his ability to capitalise on his reading by key quotations impressive. It is a scholarly piece, although his vision of being a great communicator may not have been wholly supported by this publication. I felt he allowed the need to impress dominate to the point that it led to unnecessarily difficult communication. If I may select a few points and quotations from the guide under certain of his headings in order to illustrate Robert's orientation in the projects:

Guide to the Retrospective Exhibition.

Projects 1 and 3. Vagrancy and Mental Handicap:

'The Poor Law legislation act of 1388 forbade the relief of able bodied beggars. It took 500 years for repressive and punishment techniques to be replaced by rehabilitative ones.

Cyder Ryder, Pram Factory.

Attitudes to the vagrants have changed far less than the laws. To put the "law" or "service" into operation does not carry with it the commitment or the responsibility of the man paid to do it.' Robert painted under this theme in a very poignant manner. Dispossession and defeat meant a lot to him. He spent time among 'his' vagrants, he certainly supported them and he was resentful of the lack of recognition for their plight shown by the local authorities. It was a very clear message and a straightforward project. Much the same applies to the project on mental handicap where he depicts the atmosphere of handicap and the relentless demand on parents with, inevitably, an attack on local authority, expressing anger at what he saw as inadequate provision for the handicapped and their carers. 'Though some degree of insight had developed it was still far from satisfactory at the time of this project. Today, complacency is fast replacing ignorance', and 'A handicapped child means a handicapped parent'.

Project 11. Old Age:
Robert introduces the project with a questionable flourish, producing a dazzling string of quotations that indicate a loathing of the ageing process. These include 'You have my acutest sympathy for what you delicately call the nuisance of old age,' (Kipling), and 'There is only one irreparable and cruel evil in life – old age' (Anatole France). As a finale Robert added, 'Lenkiewicz was brought up in an old age home and thought it a moving and salutary experience. It would however be difficult to dissuade him from the notion that ageing is poor coinage compared with youth and middle age.'

A handicapped child means a handicapped parent.

Project 12. Suicide:
I liked the description of this project and thought it especially helpful. Robert reveals a fascination with suicide and his interesting slant that suicide is murder by mistaken identity. That is, the person committing suicide is not so much concerned to destroy himself but, rather, the world that he lives in. Again he shows a compassionate concern for one of our long-standing social problems, that of severe depression and self-harm.

The Relationship Projects. Projects 4 - Love and Romance, 5 – Love and Mediocrity, 8 – Jealousy, 14 – The Painter with Mary, 16 – Sexual Behaviour, 18 – The Painter with Women:
These are all explorations and variants of the themes that preoccupied Robert throughout his life. Principally, that in relating to others we are, in fact, not relating to the other person but relating to our own needs mirrored in that person, and this, in turn, leads to the phenomenon of aesthetic fascism – the 'other' being as if property, with equivalent and destructive possessiveness. Of Love and Romance– 'Lenkiewicz held the view that these behaviours indicated an obsessive, pathological ruthlessness involving patterns not unlike those found in political persuasions and fascism.' Of love in Love and Mediocrity – 'This project surveyed a wide range of assumptions and expectations about human relationships. Lenkiewicz viewed

Robert's rejection of age.

many of these assumptions as foolish and unkind.' He was dealing here with his negative views on the issue of possessiveness in long-term relations and, for him, the aversive effect of the very notion of fidelity.

In later projects such as 'Mary' he personally experienced the physical impact of not being able to possess a person with whom he was besotted. He also moved the emphasis a little to reach the point where he made the claim, 'The project seemed to indicate that all sexual behaviour was auto-erotic; from marriage partners to strangers' underwear. It seemed an inherent and terrible isolation lay just under the surface...' (Sexual Behaviour). In 18, The Painter with Women (whose section in the *Guide to the Retrospective Exhibition* is the least well expressed in my view), Robert further expands his isolationist beliefs about relationships using the subtitle 'Observations on the theme of the double'. In essence his point is that, again, in relationships the other person serves a mirroring function; one relates to a mirrored version of oneself and one's own needs, not to the other person. He makes a clear statement in one of his notebooks:

> *In all our attractions, sympathies, empathies, interests — or so it appears to the painter — the 'other' can by physiological necessity only ever be a fragmented mirror. The painter may think he thinks of her, certainly; but he can only feel his feelings and think his thoughts. So he must consider where she came from — where indeed did she really come from? His first response to her was his aesthetic reaction to that alleged a priori. It is clear that she came from him and he can only embrace himself.*

I have sometimes been asked for my views as a psychologist on Robert's outlook to relationships. I will give these later but, for the moment, I prefer the luxury of a little personal musing and will comment, keeping clear of formal psychology. Curiously, in the sense that it was something that he appeared to stand against, I would say that Robert's concepts led him into being self-preoccupied and exploiting of others. But he had such a charismatic presence and an enduring ability to 'recruit' and retain women friends that he ended up, effectively, with a stable relationship to *women*, rather than a woman. It worked for him in the sense that he met basic human needs and always gained immense benefit from the ongoing experience of being cared for emotionally, physically and sexually, it seems, throughout most of his life. While individual women may have been readily substituted over the years the presence and function of the women in his life remained stable and reliable. His apparent isolationist views masked the fact that he has always had the same needs as the rest of us but met them, atypically, through multiple relationships — although this only worked because it was tolerated by others who 'worked at it' on his behalf. He was, therefore, indulged. It is not a model for relating that could be expanded to any significant proportion of our society, since inequities in personal attractiveness and charisma would lead to unworkable breakdown in the arrangement, with many left in isolation and loneliness. You would have to possess the confidence in personal allure that Robert enjoyed in order to cope with it. That is, rather than worry about how the next relationship is to be secured one simply attends, as Robert did with such confidence, to the growing queue.

The last project that I will mention is Project 17, Observations on Local Education. Robert describes the experience of working on this project (work that included collecting written comments from five hundred sitters either receiving or delivering education) as 'the least salutary and the most depressing of all the projects. It presented imagery and ideas that make the claim that contemporary education is the mass creative slaughter of the young.' Robert listed the conscripted nature of schooling, the isolating impact of large numbers of people, examinations and destructive forms of competition as devices for control in order to educate in relation to commercial enterprise. He appears to voice his disappointment and lack of respect for the professions that run education, 'The young person's sensitivity to example is

Paintings from Project 17 - Education.

Detail from The Death of Education.

immeasurable. A parent or mentor whose creative life is passionless, dulled or uninspired will have great difficulty in valuing themselves…'. In contrast, 'Sensuality, energy, and amoral curiosity frighten the adult and the adult will fear the child'. Tellingly, Robert relates an anecdote in this section concerning the explorer in the Amazon who asks a child to point out his father among the tribespeople. The child responds by striking the explorer in anger saying, 'I belong to no one, at this moment you are my father.' This catches Robert's personal creed. A creed that he projects beyond himself on to education, parenting and relationships in general – 'I BELONG TO NO ONE.'

As with many of Lenkiewicz's observations, critiques and general comments on our lives and way of doing things as a society, there is a strong element in all this that makes one stop, think and reflect, rather sadly perhaps, that he has important points. Maybe things are not so good in education, especially for the highly creative and individualistic child – the type of child that he was, in fact. Although he said little to me about it he hinted that his own experience of schooling at a Secondary Modern school was unpleasant and unhelpful, he got little from it. The education project results in him rediscovering the down side of education and the limitations he remembers within our educational process. His portrayals are often deliberately bland and dull to reflect this.

In contrast, reports from Robert's own students in later years all confirm that he was a brilliant, inspiring and patient teacher of painting skills himself. But this was at times and frequencies of his choosing and mainly on a one-to-one basis with adults, some of whom he had a relationship with anyway. How would he approach the queue of thousands of children in need of education? What a glorious experiment it would have been to have him as director of education for a while. How would his romantic notions of education have been translated into job descriptions for thousands of teachers across the disciplines, and what expectations would there have been for the broad mass of children in relation to attendance and involvement in education?

It is not my intention in this review to respond in any depth to the issues that Robert presents in these projects. Rather, to use the review as part of my claim that Robert was a man with a fine intellect. The projects were intelligently conceived from a background of extensive thought and reading. Often they were accompanied by extensive notes. Robert's *insulation* from the hard practicalities of everyday life and responsibilities may have led to curious perceptions and, many say, unworkable notions of relationships and education. Overall, though, on the basis of first-hand conversation, together with exposure to some of his notebooks and published writing, I do have full confidence in my regard for Robert as an intellect of some significance.

TRAGEDY

Other than the possession of a sharp intelligence and a preoccupation with the evolution of religious ideation through the ages, especially the Middle Ages and Renaissance era, what emerges from Robert's notes and writing is that he had a special thing about tragedy. This is evident in the focus on tragedy that Robert wrote around the illustration related to Rothko's suicide. It was, though, a very intellectual thing, with the meaning and resolution of tragedy being sought in the intellectual depths of the philosophers rather than the emotional depths of, say, person-centred psychology. In his early years, brought up in the Hotel Shemtov, Robert records having been a frequent spectator to personal tragedy. Of this there seems little doubt. In particular, the stories of the holocaust and fate of the Jewish refugee population that his parents harboured in the hotel after the Second World War will have made an intrusive and lasting impression on a young Jewish man.

Robert saw a close link between art and tragedy. In fact, Lousie Courtnell, a pupil of and sitter for Robert over many years, recounted in a public talk recently that he would say to her, 'Life is tragedy. The arts just make it more bearable.'

Curiously, embedded in a spoof critique of his own work that Robert had published in *The Times* on 14 December 1977 (under the name Paul Overy), he wrote:

> *We have gone a long way since the days when the first modern artists of the century suffered hardships. The indulged misery of Modigliani or Soutine has passed and with it the Bateau Lavoir and Bohemia. As late as the first year of this post war period there were still 'artistes maudits'. Wols died pursued by misery and De Stael suffered until his suicide. The American abstract painters battled against poverty and Klee's remark, 'The people are not on our side' was a harsh truism.*
>
> *Today the successful painters have magnificent studios and comfortable lives. In the United States to be a modern painter is to belong to a social category as desirable as that of a university professor or a president of a corporation.*
>
> Lenkiewicz writing under the pen name 'Paul Overy', 1977

This harangue by Robert continues at length before turning to an equally violent attack on his own work. *It is almost a lament at his own lack of tragedy.* In the accompanying picture he stands with his vagrant friend, Diogenes. At times he would write or comment that it was necessary to live among tragic and dispossessed people fully to appreciate their world. On occasions he did just that, taking inspiration from Gericault, who actually lived amongst his subjects at times. I once made the light-hearted point to Robert that tragedy made a compelling call to him and had earned his lifelong fascination yet, at the same time, it was ironic that the only real tragedy in Robert's life was that he suffered no true tragedy to live out himself. At this he simply chuckled and smiled acknowledgement. I was referring to the fact that he had always enjoyed support of one kind or another and had never, to my knowledge, known a period of the personal tragedy of utter loneliness, dispossession and defeat. He had generally good health until his late forties, had usually been richly provided for by female partners and associates and, other than the spell of several months in Exeter prison, what physical hardship he might have suffered was self-imposed. He flirted with tragedy but it evaded him personally until, that is, his obsession with collecting rare books ran him into such debt that he became distracted by it and spent most of his later years painting to annul debt – painting at a level that was well below that of his best works and potential masterpieces. That is a kind of tragedy, it is true, but probably more for us than him. In compensation for the lack of personal tragedy, perhaps, Robert surrounded himself with and was fascinated by the tragedy of the vagrant and alcoholic populations of London and then Plymouth. This was a vicarious experience of tragedy.

It should be noted that closely linked to his interests in religious concepts Robert also held a strong fascination for witchcraft and fanatical thought, including the persecution of so-called witches. This became evident upon the death of a colleague of mine, Lawrence Normand, who was a fellow lecturer at the University of Exeter. He was not in my department (Psychology), but belonged in the Arts Faculty, specialising in the history of witchcraft. Robert contacted me one day in a degree of agitation to ask if I could assist in saving the notes and papers concerning witchcraft that were part of Lawrence's collection. He regarded these as important and feared that these would be lost. I was happy to help and eventually handed them over to Robert who breathed a sigh of relief to have them in safe keeping. Latterly his other related interest, that is, fanatical beliefs and behaviour, tended to occupy him equally, especially with current events such as the wars in The Gulf and Afghanistan.

The burdens of knowledge.

A second watercolour from Robert's early notebooks, rather better known through various publications, distantly reflects this theme of human tragedy and the sense of burden sitting upon shoulders. But here Robert lapses into the theatrical, one might almost say embarrassingly so. He portrays himself dramatically as a figure subject to an increasing tragic load as he encounters the skills and intellect of past figures of great stature. The attached notes read:

> *How heavy is a childhood load? At eleven Rembrandt climbed up – at twelve Michelangelo, at thirteen Nietzsche; and so it went on. And that odd little trinity has balanced there – always precariously – for a long time now. Have I become bow-legged? How bow-legged could a civilisation become? A soldier, lover, painter…?*

This provides a small insight into one of the many facets of Robert's self image. He portrays himself as encountering and shouldering, custodian like, the weight of great thoughts (from great thinkers) and great paintings (from great painters). It is a dramatic assumption of the ownership of burdens. Yet there is also a modesty here in that there is no inclination to suggest that he furthers, improves or rivals anything in these fields. My view is that that is too modest. Robert certainly contributes in a powerful and idiosyncratic way, especially as a painter although not, perhaps, as a show-stopping philosopher. He was undoubtedly a very competent steward and promoter of philosophical knowledge though.

BIBLIOMANIA?

Linked to the issue of his intellect and the projects was Robert's obsession with rare books. As Michael Palmer records later, the pace of Robert's work in his last few years accelerated to a point that, I infer, it became an obvious and, ultimately, unsustainable health risk. To put this more directly, Robert progressively exhausted himself and compounded his condition of heart failure. The drive behind all this was his compulsion to continue adding to his library. It was a compulsion that was, effectively, out of control. The out of control compulsion of a *collector* is rather different from that of a compulsive gambler. The former is driven by the thrill of scale and expanding numbers while the latter involves entrapment through small wins that inflame the lure of finally winning on grand scale. The net outcome is invariably the same – serious debt. The figures will probably never be known but it is a firm belief among his close followers that Robert spent millions of pounds over the years on the acquisition of books both from the manuscript and printing eras. Things were improving, it seems, but he was seriously in debt to book dealers on his death and, unwisely, still active with acquisitions. It is sobering news that, after his death, a sale of some of his key antiquarian assets at Sotheby's led to disappointment concerning the overall value. One view is that Robert's mania for books misled him into paying rather too much for some acquisitions. I recently learned of a claim that there is documentary evidence that he paid excessively for certain assets – perhaps up to a factor of ten. Further, he 'padded out' the collection with an amount of material that was relatively mediocre or with less-valuable multiple copies. One somewhat out-of-character note from his biography records that Robert actually went to prison for some months for removing 'unused' old books from Plymouth Museum and selling them. In this case, though, it was not the love of books but more a 'Robin Hood' drama since, he claims, he sold them to raise money to feed his vagrant community.

It is a failure on my part that I never explored the issue of antiquarian books with him in any depth. In truth this was because I was not aware of the magnitude of the problem. In general he kept quiet about the situation and made little mention to me of the debt problem. Of course, the debt was not just for books. Rentals, refurbishments and other collector's items also took a heavy toll. It is clear that he especially loved the presence of these books and certainly made use of some of the religious and philosophical texts for personal reference and research. However, not reading Latin or other ancient linguistic forms, some of his collection were just a revered presence, not something that he could truly use. He was

Robert's passion.

The Polygraphia *(1517) was a thrilling catch.*

extremely excited on one of my visits because he had just acquired *The Polygraphia*, dated 1517.

Belatedly, I have asked several people close to Robert a straightforward question, 'What was it with Robert and ancient, rare books, many of which he could not even read?' They have all hesitated a little and felt their way into a speculative answer. Nick Fox, who catalogued Robert's philosophy collection, made two interesting comments to me, 'He was very acquisitive by nature anyway, and the antiquarian books added to the atmosphere he liked creating.' I checked Nick's meaning here and, as suspected, he was referring to the smell, look and general contribution the books made to Robert's simulated Renaissance environments. Also, in reply to my question about whether Robert's collection of books really did stand, as he claimed, at a quarter of a million and if so why so, Nick replied, 'He loved the scale of it all, but, to be honest, I think that he was a bit inclined to add naughts to the numbers.' There may be some links that are difficult to trace regarding books and the family background too. Having put the question to John Lenkiewicz, Robert's younger brother, he revealed that in her earlier days Mrs Lenkiewicz had a link with a blind antiquary to whom she read aloud. Apparently the man referred to her as the 'light' of his life. In Robert's special bond with his mother, old books may thus have acquired special significance.

All this having been said it would be disingenuous to leave scope for the conclusion that Robert's near lifelong effort at collecting books was frivolous and little more than an arbitrary addiction. In the introduction to the *Guide to the Retrospective Exhibition* Robert writes of his library:

Over the years he has put together a large and specialist library with many rooms. Each one contains books on a specific theme, there are rooms on Metaphysics, Philosophy, Death, Suicide and Euthanasia, Theology, Literature and Poetry and two further rooms of Art History and Art Biography. The library and the projects have in common his consistent research into the causes of obsessive and fanatical behaviour.

Clearly Robert's collector's mania with regard to books was not directionless. It was intellectually driven, linked in with his major painting projects and held the hope of revealing some basic truth to explain aspects of human behaviour that puzzled and troubled him. He was also mindful of a civic contribution in assembling a unique collection of medieval books for people in the South West of England. At one point I arranged a visit by Dr Jonathan Barry of the University of Exeter to assess some of the collection. Jonathan's view, as I recall, was that elements of the collection were second only to the collection at the British Library. Sadly much of this sustained effort by Robert is now scattered to the winds since the executor of his estate has been obliged to sell off parts of the collection to defray the debts accrued, in part, in building it up. Another irony engineered by Robert.

Having brought the issue of debt into focus, Robert's attitude to it deserves a mention. Unlike many of us he seemed to be able to avoid becoming too worried by his debts. The indications are that he judged that his alternative economy of paying in paintings what he owed would prevail. In the past he could be negligent in paying back small loans made by friends for paint and so on, taking a somewhat cavalier attitude to debt, it seems. Various letters in some of the 'aesthetic notes' were from women who mentioned being owed several hundred pounds. When he died he owed various friends and support figures various amounts, one in excess of eight thousand pounds. Meantime he let it be known that his large scale debts had reached something in the order of half a million pounds. Talking to one of his legal advisors I asked, jokingly, if Robert had tried to pay bills by giving paintings. The reply was telling, 'That would have been something, at least. He never paid his bills at all. I quickly realised that it was "extra curricula". Knowing him was the payment.'

The Theology section on the move – 2001.

ROBERT AS A SOCIAL PRESENCE

I have often been asked, 'What was he like to get on with?' Again, I have to remind readers that Robert presented different sides to different people. The following is thus very much the version of himself that he chose to give to me. Generally, he was fairly even in mood with minor shifts into a rather sunny mood if he had achieved some specific success such as a good sale of paintings. He was chatty, enjoyed conspiratorial atmospheres and often exhibited boyish excitement or enthusiasms. As an example of the latter, he revealed, on one of my visits to Mudbank, that he was thinking of a series of paintings involving clouds. He showed me one example of a cloud painting of his. On inquiry it was clear that he actually knew very little about cloud types and cloud formation. As it happens I have held a private pilot's licence for many years and, prior to that, spent quite a time gliding, so I do have a modest understanding of cloud. The result was that, for once, I reversed roles and gave Robert a fifteen minute impromptu tutorial in cloud types, how they formed and their natural history. He listened keenly and seemed to enjoy this. It followed naturally to offer him a flight with me. This he accepted with boyish enthusiasm. It is a sadness that we never actually made the trip. His health, his ever full timetable of sitters and growing pressure to produce paintings, the logistics of getting him to Exeter Airport (where the aircraft that I fly is based) on a day with suitable weather, defeated us in the end. But he remained boyishly keen, especially when I showed him a photograph of the aircraft and aerial shots of the coast and Plymouth. Perhaps the thought of Robert sitting in a Cessna 172 with headsets on while wearing his paint-covered smock was slightly ridiculous of me. A similar boyish enthusiasm was evoked when he told me of his experience driving Lord St German's quad bike in the grounds of Port Eliot. Since Robert did not drive any sort of vehicle it was a great novelty and he enthused at length about it to me. It seemed to have been a true *Boy's Own* adventure for him.

Boyish was the word, I found sometimes, when it came to food. Robert told me that he only spent some nights of the week at his cottage in Lower Compton but when he was there Anna Navas tended to his needs. This included the provision of the recommended diet for people with cardiac problems. Robert was not that keen on this diet as he intimated to me on several occasions, although he did recognise it as something approaching a necessity. A necessity, that is, that he would readily take a break from. This longing for former menus led to the following incident:

NOTES

July 1999

Breakfast at Priory Road

It has been arranged that I will visit Robert at home at about 10.30 on a Saturday morning. Because he was complaining about his diet on my last visit I have offered, conspiratorially, to bring the ingredients of a late breakfast as a brief holiday for him from diet. Lorna, my wife, is with me and has acquired some incredibly healthy venison sausages and organic eggs as a treat for Robert.

We arrive on a beautiful sunny morning and walk up through his garden to find Robert sitting outside in the sun (unusual, because he claims to hate the sun), working on a small painting. He greets the news of sausages and egg to come with great enthusiasm, as if deprived of such luxuries for, one would have thought, an eternity. Robert's stance in life is that he paints, never losing a minute. That is all he does. Therefore it falls to others around him to turn to the duties of life on his behalf. Predictably, therefore, Lorna and Anna make their way inside to deal with the breakfast while I, only slightly shamefully, settle in to the ease of the gender stereotyping and chat with Robert while the women work and he paints. A table is set on the gravestone that serves as a table top in between two bench seats. Absurdly, on the part of the three of us perhaps, the 'great man' is feted by having his breakfast delivered first. Robert jumps up from his easel and moves briskly to the table. No effort at manners and decorum is offered here for he is at his plate immediately before our food arrives – the starving schoolboy desperate to get started into his favourite food. By the time Lorna and Anna arrive with their plates and the coffee his is half finished. At one point a dish of spare sausages is temporarily placed on the ground and Robert acts in their immediate defence saying, 'don't let the cat near those', although he makes no effort to move himself to the cause. He is skittish in mood and has shown a curious, boyish impetuousness with his breakfast treat.

The 'breakfast'. Present are my wife Lorna together with Anna Navas. Note the gravestone as a table top.

When at his home as a visitor I found Robert to be conventional as a host – with the exception perhaps that after two or three hours he was clearly anxious to get on with some painting and one felt it an act of generosity to leave. In December 1998 Robert had invited Lorna and myself to Priory Road for dinner. Arriving at seven his cottage was warm and inviting with low lighting and the log-burning stove alight. I was surprised to see that there were hints of Christmas decoration around. It was a relaxed, agreeable evening with Robert who was in a mood for gentle conversation. Anna proved a fine hostess. His paintings were around and about the place and, before dinner began, I peered into various studio areas to check progress on paintings that I had seen on my previous visits. The gender stereotyping prevailed once more in that he made no moves to assist with the preparation or serving of the meal. Robert never drank alcohol but was happy enough with a bottle of wine being produced for the three of us who did.

Sometimes Robert acted with an unexpected generosity that could catch you off guard. Towards the end of the evening he suddenly produced a copy of his *The Mary Notebook* that had recently been put on sale at a price of several hundred pounds. He signed it and handed it over to me as a gift. It could have been embarrassing but fortunately (it being mid December) I had brought a small gift too. It was titled *Will Power* and had been produced by a French school of psychotherapy based in Nancy at the turn of the century. I read some extracts (it was like a recipe book of mental suggestions designed to help people achieve personal objectives – totally useless but fun) for Robert's benefit which he clearly enjoyed. Although not as substantial a gift as Robert's it saved the evening for me and, as it looked quite old, it ended up in his library.

Daytime visits to the house could be less homely in the sense that, in the winter months, it was sometimes freezing inside. On one morning I arrived to find Robert working outside on a small painting. It was a bright but cold morning and he was wrapped in a duffel coat with a scarf and a hotwater bottle on his legs. Shortly after my arrival we went inside to talk and have a coffee. If anything it was colder in the house and, despite a winter coat, by the time I left I was feeling quite shivery and was glad of the heater in the car. Robert had also departed destined for the Basement studio. This was always moderately warm I found.

Winter painting – a hotwater bottle for Robert's legs.

My other occasional sample of social Robert was at the cottage he sometimes used as a weekend retreat and an environment to inspire an entirely different type of work – his land-

A 'studio' area December 1998.

scape painting. I made just two or three summer visits to Mudbank, as it was referred to, and thought he had chosen the name well. It was a tiny cottage with, inevitably, various paintings in progress leaning here and there. Again, Robert relaxed for an hour or two as the incessant engine of creative production shut down for a little. He and I mused over the view while Lorna and Anna sorted out an early evening meal (I am sorry about falling in with this chauvinism, truly) to be taken in the late afternoon sun. He had anecdotes about night-time painting in this place, especially being startled by a badger which bumped into his leg. Because of the rather physical setting of Mudbank the conversation was often in that direction. We talked of flying, sailing, and a little of travel. These conversations were a gentle pastime – deals, building projects and Nietzsche were out of it for at least some of the visit.

In terms of bad mood, I have seen Robert tired and a little dispirited on a several occasions but never seen him angry. He was capable of anger it seems, though. An acquaintance of mine (who I regard as a thoroughly reliable observer) reported to me that he found himself walking behind Robert in the Barbican one evening. He told of an incident: 'He was in the company of one of his women who was dressed in the usual black outfit with long black hair. They did not appear to be arguing but they suddenly stopped and Robert struck her on her face.' Having reported this story to several of those close to him the consensus is that Robert could become angry but almost always controlled the anger. Thus, this incident seems very much out of character.

The view from Mudbank – Robert's romance with landscape.

There was also an incident that Robert told me of himself that, at the time, I thought betrayed an unexpectedly vindictive side. One of his assistants had taken a computer with an important client database out of Plymouth. The computer had been stolen during the trip. Robert appeared to be very annoyed about this because no back-up copy of the database had been made by her, which he regarded as negligent. From various accounts the assistant was having a hard time and getting rather stressed trying to recreate the database and was, poor soul, quite upset about it all. Robert, though, claimed to me that he possessed a personal back-up disk made without her knowledge but was not going to tell her that since she needed to learn an important lesson. Whether his possession of the back-up disk was fact or fiction I do not know, but either way it was a vindictive act or a vindictive fantasy. It did Robert no credit at all – a little supportive help would have been more appropriate.

Robert quite liked 'hobnobbing' with well known people and celebrities and making this contact known to people like myself. Amongst his 'catch' of sitters whose names he 'dropped' into our conversation were Michael Foot, Simon Callow, Jimmy Connolly, Alan Bates, Charles Dance and Pete Goss. He mentioned meeting with Britt Ekland but this did not lead to a sitting. However, his version of their conversation that he relayed to me was that she said to him, 'You are one of the most sexually attractive men that I have ever met – and also one of the most evil'. He was quite proud of this. Robert did not relate these things in a particularly boastful way, more like news-telling – but he made sure that you had heard the news.

SECRETIVENESS

Robert seemed to find great delight in building a fabric of secrecy designed to shield him from the scrutiny of those to whom he was closest or depended upon the most. I suppose it was all part of the dramatic atmosphere he loved and also linked to the cause of total freedom in sexual relationships and the provision of a situation where he could follow impulse and whim without explanation. Once I had started regular visits to the Basement studio which was, literally, the basement of a terrace house in Citadel Street in Plymouth (five minutes walk from the main Barbican studio) his love of secrecy became apparent to me. Not the least of this was the furtive way in which we seemed constrained to approach the building with an apparent need to check that no one was looking before we went down the steps and into the place. Then there was fact that if I corresponded with him on matters that he preferred not to be mentioned elsewhere ('Please do not write to my house, Keith, use this address.'), then I was to use the name and address: 'Robert Avery, Basement Flat, Citadel Road' etc. Similar furtiveness was required in my early visits to St Saviours church and at the last acquisition, the new warehouse in Castle Dyke. As for the typical secrets? I have drawn a few examples from my notes:

NOTES

20.5.1998. Basement studio:
RL: 'I have just made an excellent "paintings for frames" deal – please don't tell Esther.' (Esther Dallaway kept elements of Robert's accounts.)
'I have worked through most of the last four nights. I had to earn £30 000* urgently. Esther must not know.'

19.1.99. Prete's Café:
Robert was unusually buoyed up with excitement.
RL: 'I have just done the best deal of my life. I have offered £140 000* on a warehouse and it is going to be accepted. There must be absolute secrecy please.'
KN: 'Why all the secrecy all the time? Why not tell Esther and Anna? Tell them you are the boss – this is how it is.'
RL: 'Never, it won't work – it will be just all hassle all the way. It will be worth it when they discover it on my death.'

2.7.1999. Tudor Rose tea rooms:
RL: 'I've been on a roll with portraits for money. I've had to earn £20 000* a month for certain projects. I had to work at night but then I was ill for two weeks – it has cost me a fortune. It is essential that Annie and Esther don't find out.'
KN: 'Do you regard all the secrecy to still be necessary?'
RL: 'Yes, it remains essential. Otherwise it causes continuous difficulties.'

I then read him an extract from an article by a physiotherapist describing how chronic exhaustion preceded many heart attacks. He was interested and laughed. Then he said, 'Please don't show that to Anna.'

6.9.1999. Basement studio:
I arrive at 1.55pm to find the door ajar. I knock and Robert calls to come in. Clearly the paranoia of secrecy is waning as far as the Basement goes. I can barely get into the place. It is incredibly cluttered with dozens of paintings packed everywhere in the little room. Many paintings show signs of a recent start. Almost all are of young women except for occasional self portraits. The place looks like it is never cleaned, the floors are filthy and the kitchen area villainous. Papers, books, artefacts, paints and paintings are strewn everywhere. Only the one chair and the bed in the inner room is clear. I produce meat pies while Robert makes his usual suspicious-looking and worse-tasting cup of tea. He is bouncy and can't wait to tell some news as we settle in the inner room:

RL: 'I had to make over £100 000* and I've done it. It was a near thing. A few days ago I had a health set back. I went back to what I was like in the past – I was walking here but just taking a few steps and I was desperately out of breath. A few more and I had to stop. It kept happening. When I got here I was drenched in sweat. I took all my clothes off, lay on the bed with the fan on and slept for four or five hours, then I felt better but had to take things easy for a day or two. You must not tell Anna.' [Author's note – it sounds like Robert experienced a minor coronary event here that self-corrected].

6.2.2000. Tudor Rose tea rooms
RL: 'Please do not talk to anyone about this but I have finalised the deal on the warehouse. I will use a four year loan of £140 000 and give two paintings.'

7.12.2000. Tudor Rose tea rooms:
As I go in at the appointed time Yana Trevail comes along the street and greets me with the news that Robert is going to be late. We take a coffee together while I wait. She is chasing him to find out what he is doing since he now keeps his own diary and his movements are not well communicated, even to the trusted Yana. In reply to a question from me Yana observed:
Yana: 'Yes I have seen Robert's new building and I did see The Last Supper. Robert showed me around.'
KN: 'I thought it was all a big secret.'
Yana: 'Robert tells everyone that it is a big secret but he can't keep his own secrets for long so it doesn't stay very secret.'

How much of this was all some kind of play-acted spurious secrecy I do not know. It is quite possible that the key figures in his life did become much better informed than he let on. Even so, it was a curious habit of his and suggests the psychological mechanism of transference. That is, sometime in his earlier days an authority figure must have denied or threatened freedom such that there developed an expectation on his part that key figures would become oppressive and controlling if one revealed plans to them. Robert had unquestioningly and perhaps unconsciously transferred this expectation to people in later life, particularly women it seems. To be pragmatic in outlook it is likely that people close to Robert would have fitted his expectation, though, and tried to restrain him because his debts were mounting, his self-imposed workload was building while his health and resilience was declining. He would have given the impression that he was going to kill himself with it all – as, I believe, he did. The ladies would have nagged at the very least.

* These figures should not be taken that literally. There is often a degree of enhancement involved, as is explained in the next section

EXAGGERATION

I have placed a footnote at the end of the notes on secrecy suggesting that readers do not take the statements of financial figures in this too seriously. This is because another of Robert's consistent traits, that is reported by virtually all who knew him well, is that he exaggerated – sometimes terribly and sometimes absurdly. His numbers and values appeared to increase with the repeated telling of the story.

At times I have to confess to feeling, shall we say, mildly quizzical at some of Robert's claims. One could see that he had a habit of consolidating the future with the present and making it an entity. For example, he would often make bold claims concerning the number of paintings that he had produced. Ten thousand was a figure that he sometimes used. This has to be a record-breaking total if we are talking about *fully completed* oil paintings. My belief is that this was actually an ambition, since he dazzled himself with the scale of projected numbers. Bearing in mind that he literally had a painting life of about 18 000 days this means an average production at a rate of one completed painting in less than every two days, assuming that he painted every day of his life. In reality this was not the case. He loved painting in large scale with multiple figures. Some of these paintings will have taken hundreds of hours, as with the murals, St Antony, The Last Supper and so on. A significant number of his works remain unfinished. Is then, the total figure related to paintings started or completed? At times, estimates and hopes of the projected total number of paintings for a project seemed to become confused with the number of paintings that actually existed. I have heard him give a talk to a large audience in which he cited the number of paintings in the addiction project as standing at six hundred. But as Yana Trevail, who as an organiser of the appointments for sitters was able to track the number of paintings produced, commented, 'I don't know why he says that, there are only about one hundred and fifty so far. He plans to do six hundred.'

It is possible that if the criteria are changed from just completed paintings in oil to include all Robert's artistic products, that is, it includes pencil and ink sketches, brief watercolours, etc. the total might be ten thousand. In reality nobody that I have met seems to know exactly how many actual, finished paintings Robert produced. Does it matter? Not really. There is no doubt that he did produce thousands of oil paintings most of which are now in private hands or with the executor. Some of these are exceptional to the point of being breathtaking. That is what matters.

Another claim that leaves one a little quizzical is the oft-quoted figure of three thousand sexual partners. Again this implies some startling numbers and suggests that he needed to average a new sexual partner every five days or so throughout his life. Naturally, his life was not like that, things came in fits and starts with concentrated rushes between lapses for illness, intense work phases and a slowing related to age. I do not believe that he kept exact figures but had a favourite number that, curiously, remained unchanged during the six years that I knew him. In other words it was three thousand in 1996 and still the same in 2002. This complicates the numbers even more. Also it is not clear what he actually included in terms of physical behaviour for women to be identified as a sexual partner. Does it matter? Not really. The fact is he did secure an extraordinary number of sexual partners and was, I think it is accurate to say, adding to these even in the year in which he died.

Having said that Robert could sometimes exaggerate in an absurd way. His claims concerning the 'Fountain Woman' take pride of place. He recounted this to me in apparent secrecy but I later had it described by a contact as a 'well-circulated boast'. Most of his friends had heard it. A sexual partner of his (I have no idea who she was or when this incident was supposed to have taken place) exhibited a physical characteristic that the French refer to as being fountain women. That is, on orgasm, a quantity of fluid is expelled from the vagina by the contraction that is induced. Robert made the claim that on one extended session he counted the number of orgasms in this partner and assessed fluid production. He claims that he induced an heroic fifty-two orgasms and he put the quantity of fluid expelled (he demonstrated this to me with his hands) considerably in excess of a cubic foot. Pity the poor woman, she would have been carried out on a stretcher needing an emergency drip long before the end of the session were this so. On that particular day I left thinking that Robert had lost his presence of mind, this was absurd exaggeration. I did not get the impression, wrongly it is possible, that he was clowning around, though. The story was presented as a boastful but serious claim. I felt a little cross with him for not seeing that he was risking my respect for him by being so absurd. Maybe I showed this for, although I said nothing, there were no more such stories involving absurd exaggeration. Told in modest and realistic terms it would have been an anecdote of real interest that generated discussion. Did it matter? Not really.

'SPECIALNESS' AND THE RUSH TO POSSESS ROBERT LENKIEWICZ

On Robert's death a curious phenomenon became evident that I think can, in all reasonableness, be referred to as the rush to possess Lenkiewicz. This has been and in some ways still continues to be a spectacular and superbly ironic enactment of Robert's notions of aesthetic fascism. He spoke with such distaste on possessiveness which he considered tantamount to treating people as property. In this case, though, it is Lenkiewicz himself who is treated as the property. Early on, after his death, there was an evident sense of urgency among some of his lovers, friends, assistants, partners, commercial contacts, pupils and general help-mates who had all achieved a relationship with Robert. The urgency was to do with establishing a claim of possession – *'I had a special knowledge of him and a special relationship with him'*, and sometimes *'He was my Robert'*. On occasions I caught myself referring to this as a stampede to possess Robert.

I am not a distant, lofty observer in this respect I should say, because for a while I think that I took part in the stampede. In retrospect this should have been no surprise to me for, if I may briefly use myself as a case study, once into the cycle of regular conversations with him, I became strongly aware of the fact that Robert had an unusually interesting and powerfully seductive presence. Seductive in the sense that he had quickly fashioned our relationship so that it felt both revelatory yet, at the same time, secretive. He had a seductive way of making one feel like a privileged insider, a 'court confidant'. Our conversations had an atmosphere and content that sometimes justified the phrase 'an extravagance of intimacies', often being on intimate aspects of his life – and occasionally mine. For example, he would regularly talk of current sexual adventures and relationships, musing on his motivation for these and even reviewing his physical technique in sexual encounters as declining health intruded. He would speak in depth of his perception of and relationship with various key female figures in his life. As described above, he enacted this drama of secrecy in relation to his many and various relationships, his various money-raising activities, new book and property acquisitions, forthcoming deals, emerging plans and distant ambitions. He claimed that his inner core of female supporters knew nothing about most of these aspects of his life. 'It is very important that they do not find out,' was a familiar injunction. He promoted the sense of the naughty child trying to get away with forbidden excesses under the noses of reproving parents, with myself as a privileged observer who had somehow been selected out as bearer of this intimate knowledge.

Naturally, all this did feel very intimate and extravagantly revealing and, I have to confess, I did feel a little bit special to him for a while and was motivated to preserve this aspect of the relationship. But it was a response that he commonly evoked in people since, as time went by, I began to understand that it was a presence and a ploy that he maintained with many others apart from myself. This sense of apparently being singled out as a confidant in a manner that allowed one to feel a sense of 'specialness' had a heady effect. It could be quite thrilling. But, sadly, it was mainly illusory. Illusory because often the 'secrets' were not as secret as he intimated, and also because there were various other 'specials'. With the passing of time I became more realistic as I realised that we did have a true friendship but that it was a minor thing really. It served me because it gave sufficient contact and closeness to him to justify taking a view on him – but I was not that special. It served him because he liked engaging with male companions and found novelty in one of these being a psychologist with an interest in him. The truth of it was, though, as he regularly indicated, no one was special to him in the sense that they could not readily be substituted. Even so, on his death, my acquired detachment failed me for a while and I did feel a bit 'clingy' to the notion that I might have been a figure that had some special importance to Robert. Not so, there were probably a dozen or more in my position.

The stampede to possess Robert would have amused him and he would have derided it publicly if he could. He can make no complaint though because, although he complained of the absurdity of enduring relationships and denigrated the whole concept of love and attachment, he worked tirelessly to produce exactly such an effect in the people around him. In this sense our Robert *was* a fake (see the next section).

I now recognise that this evocation of 'specialness' was an extremely manipulative device that Robert used to ensure support and help – he recognised that he was different and knew that he had an exceptional talent that needed sheltering. My belief is that he strove to generate this kind of enduring, sometimes sacrificial, possessive support from others to create a situation of safe harbour in which he could pursue his quests. Whether this was an unconscious drive or not I do not know. The product was a situation that, on one hand, he claimed to despise (people being possessive of others) but, on the other hand, one on which he deeply depended. An exquisite conflict.

Quite a number of people that I have met or conversed with in my assessment of Robert reveal, in one way or another, that they felt special to Robert and had experienced this sense of being a privileged insider. Some are still troubled by a prevailing possessiveness that it provokes.

WAS LENKIEWICZ A FAKE?

With all this creation and enactment of theatre – the drama of the Renaissance look-alike environments, the staged offbeat humour, the incongruously combined auras of sexual excess and absent parenting, intertwined with strong social concerns and humanely oriented philosophical preoccupations – is it reasonable to level the accusation that, underneath it all, Lenkiewicz was a fake? I have argued above that I regard his whole pitch concerning aesthetic fascism to be something of a fraud. It is a fake in the sense that he effectively urges *us* to break away from our basic needs for interpersonal security and consequent stable patterns of relating to others while at the same time it is obvious that he had the same needs and met these in a way that most of us never could or would be able to achieve. *He argued against intensely possessive relationships but then worked hard to create them for his own security.*

What of wider issues though? At my first meeting with Lord St Germans (see below) I asked him what explanation he held for the fact that Robert was alienated from 'the establishment', but at the same time had made an enduring friendship with a member of the aristocracy. His reply was most unexpected:

NOTES
October 21st 2003
Lord St G. 'Because we immediately recognised one another for what we were – mutual scam artists, hustlers, frauds. We instantly recognised it in one another.'

I asked him to elaborate a little and he listed traits such as the ability to have others carry out one's wishes through sheer force of personality combined with the illusion of power within.

There is little doubt that Robert had such capabilities but does that mean he was a fake? Yes, Lenkiewicz was extremely theatrical and so created an ongoing self-focused centre of compelling theatre with a skillfully fashioned range of illusory settings. Yes, he may have embellished and exaggerated with his claims of 10 000 paintings completed, 250 000 books collected and 3000 sexual partners initiated. Yes, he pursued excessive scale, and through that a degree of attention, but was it all a scam? I think that the key point is that scam artists do not come up with the goods and thus leave their victims poorer. Whatever else one says about Lenkiewicz, in the key activities of his life he most definitely came up with the goods and has left us richer for it – at least in terms of works of art.

A brief study of his approach to the Round Room Mural has left me more than impressed with the scale, depth and sincerity of the event. The extent of the preparation and intellect behind it and the quite exceptional creativity that he demonstrated in its creation speak for themselves. I take the inference from Lord St Germans' statement that he was referring to Robert's advanced powers of manipulation (that I describe above) through which means he secured the freedom, materials, environmental, financial and domestic support to devote his life exclusively to creative output and collecting.

The key point, though, is that he came up with the goods, although he may have merited acclaim for his special skills in 'hustling' as he managed the platform of his support in the form of recruiting dozens of people who, one way or another, helped him on his way – sometimes at considerable personal cost to them.

At this point I feel that I have finished elaborating the 'statement' of my portrait of Robert Lenkiewicz. Rather like many of Robert's paintings it is not finished. The key figure is basically presented but elements of background and bits of detail here and there are absent. As it happens I've got about as far with it as he got with his painting of me (see later), so he cannot complain, added to which further detail is to be found in the following chapters.

Some of the cartoons and notes as preparations for the Round Room Mural at Port Eliot.

Some of the 'goods' – a section of the Round Room Mural.

Robert LENKIEWICZ A MEMOIR — Lord St Germans

Author's note: Lord St Germans maintained a friendship with Robert of more than thirty years standing. It was a complex relationship. Lord St Germans supported Robert in various ways while, at the same time, they enjoyed a deep and lasting social relationship. It is also the case that they functioned as co-conspirators in various events that some have labelled 'delinquent'. Perhaps of greater significance than these escapades is the thirty-year span of episodic creative labour that led to the Round Room Riddle Painting at Port Eliot – the estate house in which Lord St Germans resides. This huge mural captures Robert's exceptional mastery of figurative painting. It is undoubtedly one of his finest works. Robert was, in general, very anti-establishment and it is a curiosity that he established and maintained this relationship with aristocracy. Having questioned both of them on their understanding of why it happened, the key factor seemed to be that they both just liked one another a great deal on first contact and thence after got on extremely well. As part of this memorial to Robert it is fitting to include Lord St German's history of their relationship.

The Round Room (left) at Port Eliot.

Lord St Germans with Robert.

Young Lord St Germans and his Round Room.

Before painting began.

Marcia Sands with her portrait sketch drawn in 1975 for £3.

We met each other in our late twenties, just after Robert had started the big mural in Plymouth down on the Barbican. Shortly before I came across Robert, I had cleared one of the main rooms at Port Eliot of the accumulated furniture and the junk of a century or more. It is a perfectly portioned circular room designed by Sir John Soane some 42ft in diameter. I left it perfectly empty for a while, wondering what to do with it. To furnish it in any orthodox manner might have left the house looking as if there had been a clearance sale.

At about this time, I first became aware that Robert was working on a mural in the Barbican. It had been scaffolded and entirely shrouded by two or three huge tarpaulins, making it near impossible to get even a glimpse of what was going on behind the screen. Over the ensuing months I kept an eye on the development, enough to realise that the prefect solution to the problem of decorating the Round Room would be if Robert would paint a mural in it. So I climbed up the scaffold and asked him out on a blind date. He had no idea of who I was or where I lived.

A few days later he came over to dinner with a companion. At the end of this I showed him the Round Room. He was enthusiastic about the idea of doing a mural and it was agreed that in return for 'improving' my house I would 'improve' his by re-roofing it. We, in fact, came to a financial arrangement and I paid the rent on the Barbican studio for many years.

At that time Robert had other sponsors to a greater or lesser degree, none more important perhaps than the restaurateurs and café owners of the Barbican for whom Robert did murals in exchange, as far as I could see, for a lifetime of free food. Robert was very poor at this time. Often the electricity was cut off and the City was constantly after him for the rates. In exchange for pictures some of his patrons picked up these 'inconveniences'.

Robert was also greatly helped by some of the Plymouth city taxi drivers. Often at little or no charge they would run errands for him, here and there around the town, and would be in league with him on romantic and other escapades.

At that time, the early seventies, he was doing 'End of the Pier Portraits' in pencil for the tourists at £3 each of which he could sometimes do 40 to 60 a day. He also ran a squatting agency for the derelicts and the vagabonds of Plymouth. This infuriated the City Authorities and for a decade or two he was a constant thorn in Plymouth civic affairs, irritating awkward Councillors and challenging them to do the job for which they had been elected.

In the days when Robert was himself being a patron to the vagrants, alcoholics and street people and the like, they would occasionally run errands for him. Robert would let it be known that he needed, say, a pair of 16ft barn doors, a dozen gravestones, plus a list of contemporary art books. Within a month or two he generally had what he needed (but that was long ago).

Robert always looked the same and wore the same outfit of a fisherman's smock over dark trousers tucked into huge regulation fireman's boots. His below-shoulder-length hair was usually well kept as was his beard. Robert had the complexion that a girl would die for, pink, clear and smooth, with rather reddish lips. Wherever he went he trailed a plume smelling slightly of turpentine and acrylic.

Physically he was prodigiously strong and would frequently perform pointless feats of astonishing strength, lifting huge granite blocks or immense quantities of bricks in a home-made hod. These extremes could have put an early strain on his heart and may ultimately have killed him.

It was completely astonishing the number of balls Robert could keep in the air at any one time. Occasionally I would get a look over his shoulder and into his current diary. These were home made, often the size of a church lectern bible, usually bound between plywood or boards of oak. They contained appointments for sittings of which there could often be eight, nine or ten a day. There were pages of notes and observations on the incidents of the day. Tipped into this diary were bus tickets and snippets from the papers. Encounters with girls were recorded and countless watercolours, drawings and other graphics were scattered throughout. It is hard to imagine where the time came from to keep up with these writings.

At first during the 30 years or so that Robert worked on and off on the mural (mostly off) he would come to Port Eliot quite often. On those early occasions he would often paint 12 to 18 hours a day for three or four days at time. Later, girls would come and stay with him and he only painted 8-10 hours a day. Later still, women were banned altogether. He continued to paint only 8-10 hours a day but most days we would walk the gardens or sit for an hour or two in the Morning Room.

Heathcote Williams, wordsmith, actor, poet and sculptor was living and working here during the 80s and early 90s, and there were lively conversations over dinner together. Robert's immense scholarship and philosophical disposition would come face to face with Heathcote Williams' dazzling mental agility and almost total recall of everything that he had ever read. It was a joy to listen to them both. Robert could be a bit of a dry biscuit on occasions, but, sensing such moments, he would often leaven the situation by telling Central European Jewish jokes that were cleverly to the point. Since Robert considered himself more of an illustrator than an artist and my interest lies in artefacts rather than Art, we seldom talked about the process of Art. Anecdotal trivia, gossip and scandals involving artists throughout Art's history featured in our conversations. This combined with my interests in how things work and theories on gardening were some of our constant chitchats.

Robert had many relationships with dozens of women. Along the way there were several emotional shipwrecks, heartaches and catastrophes. It should be pointed out none of them were Robert's. To the best of my knowledge, of those women I got to know, all appeared to have benefited from their encounter with him.

I cannot comment on his relationship with his children. From time to time we would exchange the usual anguish of parents with children passing through the tiresomeness of youth, and at others we'd take pleasure in their achievements.

Robert working at night on the depiction of Moses in the Round Room Mural, 1980.

At night, working on a drape by Moses' right hand, 1980.

Robert with the mural (left and above) as it encompasses the fireplace, 1980.

The Fall from Grace.

Preparatory notes and sketches.

Moses and the drape.

BOOKS

Robert's last project was an inquiry into the nature of addictions. He had one himself, Bibliomania, which on one occasion deprived him of his liberty for a while. When I first saw his books in the early 70s I noticed at that time a large proportion was made up of copies of manuscripts in various libraries around the world. To call them copies is to under-estimate the care taken with them, they were more of a facsimile than a copy.

Towards the end of his life there were tens of thousands of books in his library. He would do paintings or watercolours in exchange for this or that book and then exchange those with dealers for another item. That was one of the ways he accumulated books. It remains a mystery to me by what other means he got books. It gave him great satisfaction that scholars from Europe and America had used his library for their own research. Occasionally Robert would ask me to let his visitor see the manuscripts here.

Robert with a few of his prized books at his house in Priory Road, year 2000.

STUDIOS

Over the years Robert used many studios, some legally occupied, some squatted. Some were very untidy but not with the wanton abandon that Francis Bacon kept his studio. There was a theatrical element in the studios to the extent that it might have seemed as if a Disney set designer was dressing a screen for 'The Sorcerer's Apprentice', or that of the studio of a megalomaniac artist. Either way his studios could stop you dead simply by taking a measure of the sheer volume of work on display.

One of a half dozen of Robert's studio areas in the Barbican studio.

Apart from scores of finished and unfinished works that could be seen in stacks against the wall, there was another whole set not on view. As scenery backdrops rise up into 'flies' at the theatre, so Robert had carefully cobbled together a similar arrangement above the ceiling into which a score or more of other large canvases could be raised between the trusses of the roof construction. These could be raised and lowered by ropes depending who was coming for the next sitting. It was a 'tidy job'.

The Barbican studio was an open studio. Anybody could and did just ring the bell and walk up into the studio. There were seldom many books in it but there was always a bewildering amount of abandoned artist's palettes in a dozen places round the studio all seemingly scattered at random, and a score or more of glass jars filled with brushes. To be in the studio any length of time was to be awed by the magnificent obsession Robert had with his life. He and I would chuckle about that too.

ESCAPADES

1. Renaming the Alley

When Robert started out on one of his many escapades, he prepared them well. The jokes always took enormous amounts of time in the planning and, on occasion, huge physical effort. Some might consider that he did this for self-aggrandisement. Be that as it may, there was, however, always a very seriously considered point to these projects.

One of these involved Robert who had long campaigned and lobbied the City Fathers for the better understanding of alcoholism in Plymouth. There is an alley between his Barbican studio and the adjacent building some three feet wide and forty feet high. One of the studio doors is set back a little and opens directly on to the alleyway. On its wall the alley has a nineteenth-century iron black-on-white sign some ten feet off the ground, proclaiming it to be 'Basket Ope'. During the first ten years or so of Robert's occupation of the studio, people passed to and fro without much disturbance to Robert. At that time there were eight or nine places where alcohol could be bought on and around the Barbican. Almost overnight another two dozen or more liquor outlets were licensed and appeared within the same area. This was something Robert found deeply depressing. It caused him much personal revulsion.

On most nights and especially at the weekend the little alleyway became a vomitorium, uni-sex urinal and general fuck hutch. It was known locally as 'Piss and Puke Alley'. When it rained, it was not unusual for sludge and slime to ooze into the studio, around and under the side door. Robert had the words 'Piss and Puke Alley' translated into twenty or thirty languages. Apart from the more obvious ones they included Sanskrit, Semaphore, Middle English, Morse Code, Mandarin, Caldean, Nordic Runes and Latin, Greek and Hebrew. He copied out the translations in an exact replica of the nineteenth-century street sign and then had them fixed to the original. There they would stay for weeks until removed by council workers. One day when the council's men were removing a sign for the umpteenth time, one of them approached Robert and said 'Oh Mr Lenawits, don't you worry, you'm a mighty fine gentleman, us has all your signs up on the walls in our cuddy.'

Today by law there is no street drinking on the Barbican. It can't be said that this was solely due to Robert's amusing and irritating attempts to point the City Fathers at an increasing social problem on the Barbican but it certainly contributed.

2. *Faking His Own Death*

The escapade that caused the most controversy was Robert's attempt to feign his own death. He was fascinated by death and well acquainted with the process of death and dying. As a child, his mother ran a hotel for elderly Jewish refugees from Hitler's Europe. From an early age he had helped his mother with the laying out of the residents as they died, and at night he would dissect mice and draw them. His house and studio were filled with *memento mori*, including a unique crystal skull, beautifully-lettered tombstones and macabre book bindings. The extent of his extraordinary library showed a depth of interest in the many aspects relating to death together with manuscript observations of his own on the matter.

He came to the conclusion that if he could go no further with his understanding of death without dying, then the next best thing was to be considered dead by everyone else, friends, family and children included. If this was to be pulled off convincingly, it required secrecy and, where appropriate, deceits.

Firstly, he had to establish over a period of many months that he was becoming ill, yet continue working on the current project on 'Still Lives'. Before I became a co-conspirator I remember slight but not grave feelings of concern about his health, through the casual mentioning of, say, that he had had a fainting episode or the need for a rest between A and B when walking on the streets of Plymouth. Gradually he took accomplices into his confidence on a need-to-know basis. My role was to provide the temporary tomb at Port Eliot.

When everything was ready he had reluctantly allowed himself to be persuaded to make an appointment to see a heart consultant in London. This appointment was made through his brother who is a consultant in another medical discipline. The first that anyone knew that Robert had 'died' was a small notice in the 'Deaths' column of the Plymouth *Evening Herald* on 3 February 1981. The studio was closed and left in the capable hands of Miriam whose ancestors came from the high Colombian Andes. She had a tranquil grace about her, largely due to a wonderful deportment. Small, but with long limbs and fingers, she had a ready smile yet her face in repose was one of abject despair. There are several pictures of her by Robert showing her to have had an extraordinary beauty. Incredibly she held the line against all comers with the apparent dignified grief of someone in deep mourning. She patiently dealt with the remorseless questions, threats and stress from the media and concerned friends, acquaintances and relatives who flocked to the door.

Meanwhile Robert was holed up in a darkened room at Port Eliot and everyone else imagined him dead. Almost at once there was a local media frenzy followed within 24 hours by the nationals. Robert had informed the city police of what he was going to do and when the hacks got on to the police they were informed that 'the police were satisfied with their inquiries' and not a word more came from them.

In the house, Robert painted a self-portrait and worked in the Round Room and made notes. He also listened constantly to the local radio stations that were jammed up with obituary tributes, anecdotal/biographical incidents from the fans, and diatribes from those who had never had anything pleasant to say about Robert. Robert listened to all this and I think he was surprised by the extent of the frenzy. Afterwards, on a couple of occasions, Robert was whacked by those who were outraged by the false suffering they had gone through on his behalf.

Within three days of death, a coroner with the full majesty of the law becomes involved and requires that the body be shown to him or his representative. So to avoid having to be exposed, we had concocted a plan to raise Robert from the dead by smuggling him into the studio in front of approximately forty photographers, journalists and three TV crews. He was to miraculously appear from within the besieged studio building, which had been scrupulously examined by the hacks and declared Lenkiewicz-free. The Estate had a Ford Transit van at the time for taking building materials around the place. With ladders and a few scaffold boards on the roof we set off in this van to Plymouth with a clear plan of what we were going to do. It went like clockwork, as if it had been rehearsed again and again.

Robert's studio is situated in a wide cul-de-sac, so that if an inadvertent motorist turns into it they have to make a three-point turn at the end to get out of it again. While doing the reversing section of the turn, a vehicle has to be backed almost up to Robert's studio door before moving forward again. The Estate van when backed up to the studio door was taller than the studio door, consequently Miriam was going to be able to open the doors at the precise moment Robert released himself from the back of the van. An hour or two prior to Robert's appointed 'resurrection' we turned into the cul-de-sac. The media pack were standing and sitting on a low wall on the opposite side of the road to the studio. It was over in a blink. If the media noticed anything at all it they would have seen a couple of dozy-looking builders taking the wrong turn into a no through road and having to make a three-point turn to get out; something that occurs all day at that spot.

At the appointed hour Miriam opened the doors and the entire media pack squeezed into the studio space, which was much smaller in those days. Robert appeared and addressed the audience for a while. Then, realising he had no 'out' he inwardly panicked and, asking to be excused a moment to go to the lavatory, he left the building with no plan in his head and locked the door behind him with the only key. My secretary, out of curiosity and unbeknown to us, had driven into Plymouth to see what was going to happen. She had parked her car in the cul-de-sac and, on seeing Robert coming out of the studio in a bit of a fluster, she opened her door. Robert got in and got clean away.

Meanwhile, in the studio outrage turned to panic as there was no way of getting out.

Miriam was assaulted and a local TV front man was caught on camera hitting a woman journalist. They were stuck in there for twenty minutes or so. Later that evening Robert returned to Plymouth to face the music.

3. Body snatching – Diogenes.

Diogenes was a picture-postcard kind of tramp. Barely the five foot two inches he claimed to be, he was petite in every sense. Thick grey whiskers surrounded his pointy face and flowed out from under a rather oversized flat cap. This gave his small face a deceptive fullness. His eyes were big, round, with strong pale blue irises and bright clear whites. A huge Kaiser Bill moustache covered his mouth. Diogenes had beautiful tiny little hands with which he had once made a living as a flyweight boxer around the West Country boxing circuit.

Of the legion of tramps that Robert took under his wing during the early 70s Diogenes was the only one to find a permanent role in his entourage. He was undoubtedly an asset to Robert. He would mind the studio door when Robert was out and about the town. Sitting picturesquely outside the Barbican studio selling postcards and posters, he would regale tourists in an impenetrable West Country accent, with little regard to syntax or grammar and tell them all sorts of lies. He would tell friends and acquaintances in which café Robert could be found. Creditors and city councillors he could generally send on their way in a state of utter confusion. Diogenes was not a fool.

Robert with Diogenes.

Robert held many examples of *memento mori* in his library and studios. He considered that there could be no more powerful a reminder of death than to have an actual cadaver to contemplate. He had arranged with Diogenes who, incidentally, was delighted with the idea, that when he died, Robert could have his body with which to do what he liked. The requisite papers were prepared and signed by both parties.

Diogenes eventually died of old age in a Plymouth hospital with Robert at his bedside. To the astonishment of all in the ward, hardly had the death rattle stopped before Robert wrapped Diogenes in the hospital sheets and carried him out on his back to an awaiting car – and away they both went. However strange this may seem, Robert had made sure that all his actions and paperwork, then and later, were, in fact, completely legal and appropriate. The body was taken to a highly esteemed embalmer.

After the embalming process a body is rendered completely inert, possesses no health hazard and is permitted to be kept above ground. Eventually Diogenes ended up in a glazed coffin exquisitely made by a violin maker of Robert's acquaintance. This was cunningly built into one of the Library bookcases. There the matter might have rested but for the Plymouth Public Health inspectorate, which seemed to be staffed by a branch of fundamentalist Evangelical Christians. Someone in that department became completely apoplectic by the idea of having a body not under the control of the authorities. 'It is the Devil's work.' they said.

If I remember correctly, a Public Health Inspector does not have jurisdiction over bodies on the public highway but only within the curtilage of buildings. This titbit of information gave Robert the idea for one of his finest escapades. At that time amid a great deal of speculation, nobody knew where the body rested. The authorities insisted that they must have possession of the body but could only make this claim if they could find the body somewhere within their jurisdiction. Robert stood on firm ground with regards to the law in this area and thwarted all endeavours by the Health Authority to obtain the body, relishing their attempts to do so.

Robert enlisted and briefed a woman friend to ring the 'Evangelical' in City Hall and spin him a yarn about how her son, having fallen under the spell of that terrible Mr Lenkiewicz, had become involved in an unmentionable and hideously macabre situation. She was ringing to tell him that she knew that her son was going to be bringing 'that tramp's' body down from somewhere off the Moor and it was going to be taken to the studio at 4pm the following day. Remembering where the Public Health Inspector's remit lay, it meant he could not intercept us while we were in transit with the body.

To our dismay the Public Health Inspector had taken up a watching position opposite the studio at 10am. The coffin was in the back of the Estate van, prepared for a midday delivery. Nevertheless, we had to continue with the plan. With the same kind of misdirections employed by conjurers we managed to unload the vehicle without the official noticing a thing and I drove away. The man from the ministry bounded forward and entered the studio. On the floor in front of him lay the coffin. At that moment of personal triumph for the civil servant, Robert jumped out of the coffin displaying a placard that read, *Habeas Corpus*, 'I have the body'.

Well, this little incident almost got out of control. It was reported in at least seventy different newspapers and around the world on TV. *The Times* even had a leader on the subject titled 'Tramp in Aspic'. There were journalists all over the place, putting even more pressure on Robert as to the whereabouts of the body. Eventually Robert decided that if he were to give an exclusive to one paper the heat would drop, and the journalists would disappear. The paper chosen was the local Plymouth *Sunday Independent*.

In order to give absolutely no clue to the selected journalist as to where the body actually lay, a further elaborate scam had to be planned and prepared. This involved two attractive women and a large limousine. All the windows in it had been blacked out with dark blue velvet and the driver was partitioned off in a same style. In the back there were exotic cushions and fancy rugs with soft interior lights. At the appointed hour the car drew up at the studio door. Robert contrived to make the journalist open the door and leave the building ahead of him. On doing so he was confronted by two vampish and ravishingly beautiful women who gently helped him into the car. Robert got in and they were driven around for an hour. They talked through the Diogenes episode together until the car stopped at the place where the body was kept. The car was parked extremely close to the building such that, on opening the car door, the door to the house was scarcely three feet away and open, leading straight into a brightly lit hallway. The rear door of the car was opened by one of the

Part of the Barbican Mural.

two exquisite women who alluringly lent forward to help the hapless journalist from the car. He was thunderstruck by her appearance and any opportunity of his looking about for clues to his whereabouts was completely lost as he was gently hustled from car to house by the two giggling girls. Having seen the body, the same quasi-erotic procedure was gone through again to return the hack to Plymouth. He never knew that it was less than half a mile between the studio and the resting place of the body and that he had merely been driven up and down the bypass for an hour or so.

4. Ducks on the Wall

A few months after a Marcel Duchamps exhibition in Plymouth had closed, Robert played his own little 'art lark'. After weeks of meticulous planning and with a well-marshalled crew of about twenty, Robert erected scaffold entirely to cover the Barbican mural. As the scaffold grew rise-by-rise, so a team of helpers followed behind painting over the mural with child's white poster paint. By the time the scaffold was fully up, the painters were fifteen minutes or so from completing their job too, whereupon the scaffold came down and was neatly stacked away.

Earlier that week Robert had made three huge low-relief papier mâché flying ducks complete in all their glory, with a high-gloss polychrome, full colour finish. These were fixed to the wall whilst the scaffold was up. This entire operation was completed during a single night.

The Ducks on the Wall.

The next morning the mural had vanished. Robert sat all day beneath this homage to kitsch, canvassing votes from passers by as to whether people preferred the flying ducks or would they like the mural restored. It was April the First that day.

The Riddle Mural

Additional Author's note: It is Lord St German's intention to open the Round Room Riddle Mural to public viewing at some time in the future. Currently he is working to preserve the large collection of Robert's preparatory notes, drawings and watercolours that accumulated at Port Eliot during the thirty years while the painting was in production. Lord St Germans is also preparing a full history and commentary on the work. I asked him for a preliminary statement on the concept of the painting and why it is so called:

The mural depicts 'The Condition of Man' where one half is a representation of loneliness, unrequited love, corruption, insanity death, decay, destruction and mayhem, whilst on the opposite side there is an interpretation of harmony, proportion, love, art, truth and beauty, hope passion and friendship. Slyly included through the entire painting are veiled inferences pointing to deeper, darker and dangerous obsessions which further the conundrum of a work that Robert referred to as The Riddle Mural.

Lord St Germans
2 June 2004

The completed depiction.

Robert's early 'statement' of Lord St Germans in the mural.

The depiction of Lord St German as seen above the door in the Round Room.

Another section of the Riddle Mural.

Lord St Germans with detail from the mural, June 2004.

Detail from the mural.

Preserving the preparatory notes and watercolours.

Detail from the mural.

Detail from the mural.

85

Robert AND THE AUTHORITIES
A HAPPENING AT PLYMOUTH MUSEUM

The chapter by Lord St Germans says much about the tension that existed between Robert and authority. It was long standing. He told any who asked of his eviction from London by the police. His habit of breaking into empty premises and setting up refuges for the homeless and street-dwelling alcoholics became intolerable for the law it seems.

This preoccupation with the dispossessed dated back to early years. He was brought up in Hotel Shemtov with a mainly elderly clientele most of whom, he records, were refugees. This gave an unusual exposure to old age, psychological disturbance and death. But Robert somehow became angry about the situation of those who lived on the street and those who were addicted to alcohol. When I asked him about the origin of this anger he told me of an incident at his home during a well-attended Passover supper in which, as part of the ritual, the rabbi present called for a beggar to be brought in to be fed. Robert claims that he rushed out to a cluster of vagrants that he knew to be living under nearby arches and brought one of them into the house. However, this was not the idea it seems, a symbolic beggar in the form of a respectable neighbour was preferred and so the unkempt and rather evil-smelling man was quickly ushered out again. Young Robert was outraged and horrified by this act and later crept to his mother's fridge, stole a chicken and other food, sought out the vagrant and gave him the food with an apology. The anger at this incident and his empathy with the humiliation of the vagrant still lingered with Robert as he told me the story some 55 years later.

During a good proportion of his life he felt a transferred anger towards the authorities for their indifference towards the dispossessed and acted out this anger in various incidents of non-compliance and, I suppose, civil disobedience. Not the least of these was his habit of setting up refuges for vagrants in unoccupied premises that were not in his ownership. As the years passed his hostility to authority mellowed somewhat, leading to a curious and rather warming event in March 2000.

NOTES
12 March 2002

A reception has been arranged for the hand over of St Saviours Church to Robert and the Lenkiewicz Foundation. Robert has been generous and invited me to the reception although I have played no part whatsoever in anything to do with the Church other than being an early visitor and adding to the atmosphere of clandestine enthusiasm.

12 March: The day itself was rainy and rather unpleasant so it was nice to get to the Museum fairly early and find the gallery already made ready for the reception with Yana, Esther, Annie and Anna fussing around Robert rather like tug boats preparing a liner for departure. Lorna was with me and, whilst we were waiting for events to start, we looked around the two gallery rooms with idle interest. There was an exhibition on but I have to confess that it provoked little interest for me. I seem to have become rather rigidly Lenkiewiczian in my tastes. Unusually, we started with food and wine, which made a nice half hour. We were then ushered to seats to hear the speeches.

Viv Pengelly, one of the Plymouth City councillors, began with a greeting for all and then invited the Mayor of Plymouth to make his address and presentation. I must say that I had been eyeing the Mayor with some reservation but, almost as soon as he began talking, I warmed to him. He, again, extended greetings to the assembled dignitaries and company, finally ending with a just perceptible but deferent bow to Robert at the point where he said, 'Ladies and gentlemen and – Sir',

Robert's associates - Anna Navas, Esther Dallaway, Yana Trevail and Annie Hill-Smith.

the sir being addressed to Robert with his little bow and smile. The mayor had the air of the universal father about him, kindly and approving with a sense that his approval mattered. He spoke of Robert warmly although did admit that there was a, 'love him or loathe him division, but wherever people are on this dimension, they never ignore him.' He spoke of Robert's presence in the City being something that continually generated interest. He believed that Robert provoked thought and also appreciation of the arts; his presence in the city was valued. There was a list of achievements and I thought that the Mayor almost but not quite got to the point of saying that 'he may be a nut, but he's our nut and he keeps the cash registers ringing'. There was certainly recognition that tourism in Plymouth now owed some debt to Robert's reputation and products. I'm not sure how this fits with Robert's current self-image but it would have been something greeted with some ambivalence in the past.

In a sense, the Mayor's speech was the more seminal moment of the proceedings for me in that it felt like a paternal acceptance of what had been a rejecting child. I know a little of Robert's relationship with his own father. Lenkiewicz senior was, as Robert described him to me, remote and incommunicative but had great skill in stating disapproval with a brief, dismissive glance. Robert's early days in Plymouth were stereotypical in the sense of a young man rejected by his father who then related to the older established males of the City with a rather harsh, aggressive rejection of his own. As the Mayor smiled warmly and created a rather fatherly atmosphere, there was a sense of Robert being cherished within the 'family' and of Robert accepting this bond. It was a nice moment.

Robert with the philosophy section in St Saviours.

The Mayor rounded off and made his formal handover presentation of the Church to Annie Hill-Smith who received it on behalf of The Lenkiewicz Foundation. Robert was then called upon to reply to the Mayor. He stood up, paused erect and strode to his lectern. He was rather formal and serious in manner and initially introduced us to the Church and its contents. Slides were shown of the church and its various shelves with the philosophy section, theology section and so on. It looked impressive and the audience were appreciative. Robert then outlined plans for a grandiose development to provide a Lenkiewicz gallery. It was to be of semi-circular design and graced by the largest circular stained-glass window in the United Kingdom. He drew a sketch of the building for us using an overhead projector.

At this point, Robert drew himself up to his full height and most imposing stature (and it is quite imposing) and stared in a sweeping and rather challenging way at we in the audience. He then launched into a brief exposition of his views on the central role of physiology in fanaticism, addiction and aesthetic appreciation. He dismissed psychology, sociology and behavioural science in general as peripheral and inconsequential endeavours in relation to understanding these human tendencies. True understanding, Robert believed, was to be found at the physiological level and this was why he organised his paintings into projects which made a fundamental comment on this, the physiological position. I thought it was great fun, especially to see the audience bracing themselves, slightly transfixed by the power of Robert's assertion, almost as if they felt they had done something wrong. It left in my mind, though, the usual question mark that is familiar to me from previous conversations with Robert on this theme. Namely, what exactly is it that Robert means by physiology? He never elaborates. Is he talking about electrophysiological process, neurological process, endocrinological process, processes at a near molecular level, or is the reference to the status of major organs and systems such as the intestinal and cardiovascular system? Does Robert know his Sympatho-Adreno-Medullary system from

Robert, flanked by the Mayor's wife receives the Church building.

Plans for the new gallery.

'It is all physiological addictions'.

A symbolic moment – slicing the top off the tower.

his thyroid gland? I suspect his knowledge of these is roughly equivalent to my knowledge of fine art, that is, prone to disappoint observers. For me the debate has little edge because the psychological and physiological are so intimately involved that to separate them out to declare one of them predominant makes little sense. It is a detail, let Robert perseverate on this, his favourite theme, for as long as it entertains him. Meantime the guy can paint like God's special envoy and that's all that matters.

The proceedings ended with the audience clustering round a rather impressive cake that had been made as a model of St Saviours. Robert was called upon to cut the first slice. He bent over and chose to slice off the top off the west tower, the highest sector of the building. I was sensitive to the possibility that there might be some unconscious symbolism in his choice of which bit of the Church to attack. The thing is, he sliced the top off the best phallic symbol that the Church offered. How best to interpret this? Was he demonstrating that he had finally subdued ('castrated') the male elders of the City who for years had persecuted him? Was it an expression of anxiety that absorption into the establishment was leading to a loss of sexual and social potency, or was it perhaps a statement about age and declining personal and sexual powers? I have to confess that I had to hold back a snigger as the irreverent thought crossed my mind: 'Nah – it's just physiological. That's as far down as his arms will reach.'

LENKIEWICZ AS A PAINTER

On what basis is a painter like Lenkiewicz judged to be successful, exceptional or a master? It is an academic debate that belongs elsewhere save, perhaps, for one point. As the histories are told, painters who are held to be masters today, Courbet for example, went to their deaths unrecognised and often in poverty. Recognition came later. Recognition is about fashion to a large extent and fashion is arbitrary. A painter with exceptional skill and creative talent who has an approach that is out of fashion waits in vain for recognition.

In this context, if Robert Lenkiewicz had a burden it was that his style of classical figurative painting has been out of fashion in Britain for the last few decades. In fact, he was determinedly and spectacularly lacking in accord with the tastes of an inner core of artists and critics, mainly based in London, who determine the traffic of acclaim and fashionability in British art. At one level this did not appear to bother Robert too much. He loved figurative painting in the classical style and did not have a shred of interest in shifting style to suit fashion and attract positive comment from former detractors. Annie Hill-Smith, chairman of the Lenkiewicz Foundation, remarked in a BBC Radio interview ('Front Row' 11 September 2003) that she was fairly sure that Robert's isolation from mainstream recognition left him untroubled. I believe that she was wrong in this judgement. At times he did show chinks of regret at rejection by his true peers. Three particular replies to direct questions from myself are the basis for this comment:

NOTES

19 November 1996 KN: 'Where does your painting stand at the moment in the British scene?'
RL: *'I am dismissed.'*

20 May 1998 KN: 'You are clearly influenced by many of the great painters. Are you able to rank yourself among them?'
RL: *'No, it is not so. I will never be recognised as a great painter.'*

1 February 2002. KN: 'Does it trouble you that you are best known in the South West and not London?'

A typically 'unfashionable' portrait – Patti Avery in Blue Dress.

RL: *'I think that I know my place in the natural order of things.'*

Regret or not, Robert did not for one minute falter in his relentless production of figurative paintings.

Few people like all of Robert's paintings but most agree that there are a good number that are truly brilliant in terms of composition, idea and execution. Robert was happy to tell all inquirers that, early on, he was inspired by various classical painters such as Rembrandt, Leonardo da Vinci and Michelangelo, especially the large scale works of the latter. Also that the large-scale paintings of horses by Stubbs, the landscapes of Turner and the French Romantics, particularly Courbet and Gericault, all had a strong influence in the development of his style. He was particularly influenced by these last two painters, he recounted, and accepted that the large scale of their paintings gave him a sense of inspiration and direction. Furthermore, Gericault's morbid preoccupation with death resonated with Robert's disposition.

NOTES
19 January 1999

RL: 'I have always had a thing about large-scale works of art. Courbet's 'The Studio of the Painter' impressed me greatly, as did Gericault's 'The Raft of The Medusa'. This magnificently huge painting, The Raft of The Medusa, serves as a metaphor for society. It tells a story of a struggle for survival against starvation, cannibalism, fear and death. I have exploited large canvases and murals because they allowed me to feel like Courbet and Gericault did when they painted. Gericault would make hundreds of sketches related to a painting of this type.'

His personal history as revealed in the book *R.O. Lenkiewicz*, suggests that, as a student, he developed under his own direction. He never mentioned any influential tutors at the Royal Academy or elsewhere. In his autobiographical accounts one feature that stands out is the sense of artistic self-determinism that was evident from his quite early years. His bedroom was a studio and he held his first mini exhibition in this (at the Hotel Shemtov where he was brought up) at the age of fourteen. As some of his early pieces show he had a natural aptitude to catch form, light and tone using oils and brushes and also had advanced abilities in drawing at quite an early age.

Many people with whom I have spoken believe that Lenkiewicz was one of, if not the best figurative painters in Britain in the last three decades. It is true that, latterly, he became increasingly distracted with the problem of servicing burgeoning debt resulting from the purchase of rare books. Consequently, he tended to function in various modes. An increasingly prevalent mode was that of 'quick fire' paintings for prints, fund raising or bartering deals. In comparative terms this was highly competent work but Robert regarded it as nothing exceptional. In fact on one painting that was later sold as a print he embedded the word 'kitsch' amongst the tassels of a woman's shawl suggesting that he regarded his paintings of this type with a degree of derision. He may well have experienced a degree of professional ruefulness about the predominance of this type of painting in recent years in that it was very much below his technical and creative capabilities. Robert commented (19 January 1999) that, 'Courbet was also compromised by debt. He too would give way to producing "Pot boilers" to keep the debts at bay.' – suggesting that he took comfort from the fact that Courbet was similarly placed.

A second but increasingly less prevalent mode of painting was to do with the ongoing Project 20 that dealt with the theme of addiction. He did not discuss the falling away of commitment to this type of work with me but as Yana Travail would comment (e.g. June 2000), 'He spends most of his time on private work in his private studios these days.' It was not that he had lost interest as such but financial demands became ever more dictatorial and painting for rapid sales took on priority. But the great painter in him was not lost because he had a third mode of painting to which he still gave considerable time. In this mode he produced joyously beautiful, complex and exceptional paintings such as his The Last Supper – a painting that I feel marks him out as a master of figurative painting; it is my certain favourite.

Early self portrait (at age 17).

Details from The Last Supper.

The Last Supper.

Overall it is probably clear by now where I stand in terms of an evaluation of Robert's paintings. Thus, rather than give space to further personal comment on Robert's skill and success as a painter, a better general perspective will be provided in a review of comments from a wider range of sources. Set out below are evaluations that include figures of national or regional significance in the art world and also figures with no professional background or training in painting but just 'speaking from the heart'. I have found that assembling the following 'collage of views' helps in ordering my own reactions to his work:

David Lee (art critic) talking of the painting 'The Bishop and the Painter – Dancing to Mahler' on BBC Newsnight 18.09.03

It is a very ambitious picture, extremely ambitious. How many painters can you think of now who would be capable of painting convincingly in an interior, with so many figures as this? Only Lucian Freud springs to mind. It is beautifully painted too. I've always considered Robert Lenkiewicz to be one of the most interesting of contemporary figurative artists, he was capable of painting incredibly well and incredibly badly, like all painters.

He was not taken seriously because he was a figurative painter in a traditional, conventional style at a time when an artist who switched a light on and off won a major award. Not a single major national or regional art collection has ever given him a full retrospective so that we can see his best work and gauge it for what it is.

The Bishop and the Painter – Dancing to Mahler.

The beautiful image.

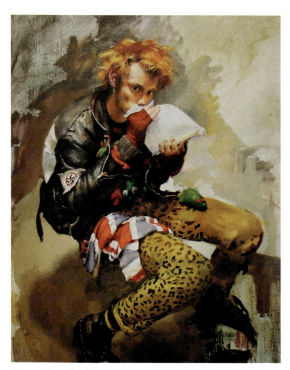

The Glue Sniffer.

Curator of a university art collection at a seminar on Lenkiewicz

I recognise that he is a talented painter but I don't like Lenkiewicz's work. I find it frightening. I would not have one of his paintings in my house.'

Sally Moore – artist and figurative painter

Lenkiewicz's technique is amazing in the sense that he is capable of painting in near photographic mode yet he goes beyond the photographic. With some painters you think 'why bother, take a photograph' but Lenkiewicz adds something exceptional and draws attention to important issues. A stunning example of this is the painting called The Glue Sniffer. One is drawn by the boy's eyes – the eyes of a beautiful toddler. Yet parts of the portrait are unfinished leaving you with a feeling of the loss of the child and possible total loss of the young man. His series on handicapped children and their mothers, and also the vagrants, are beautiful because he transmits feelings of care. He showed his care and concern and made me think differently about them through the paintings. He adds human meaning.

What I like least in his work is that in his figurative work with women he almost always chooses to depict young women who are conventionally beautiful and glamorous, there are not many middle aged or older women. He seems to choose men for depth and character and women for sexuality, it is not very mature. Conversely, the only 'beautiful' man he portrays is himself – presenting an almost Christ-like image of himself 'haloed' by his hair. In portraits of other men imperfections are shown but he seems not to look for them in himself. Having said that, the sexuality in his paintings is honest with issues like masturbation, orgasm and that very disturbing picture of a rape scene. Some of his paintings are gallery paintings rather than for the home; they really are quite disturbing.

For me he excels in the portrayal of light. His paintings are often modern but he adds classical techniques of light and shade with great skill.

As for your comment that some people complain that the figures in his paintings are all isolated, that is, they are together but do not interact and also that he is self-obsessed with so many self-portraits and portraits including himself – I think that it is all to do with sitters. Often the only sitter a painter has is himself in the mirror. In a big picture like St Antony I expect he only had one sitter at a time so interaction is difficult to portray.

Gillian – who browsed through the catalogue of the Bearne's Lenkiewicz auction

Some of these paintings are really quite ghastly.

Author's note: she was referring to pieces in 'personal language' style.

Interview transcripts Newsnight 18 September 2003

John Tedesco (of Prete's Café, the Barbican, Plymouth where Robert had painted a mural on the inner wall of the café). BBC Newsnight 18.09.03

When we unveiled it and looked at it we didn't believe then that it was The Last Supper, he had to explain it to us, over a period of time. At that time, being a very busy holiday tourist sort of area, people came in, didn't like it. I would say 99 per cent of people didn't like it, they often commented about no one smiling.

The mural in Prete's Café.

Michael Foot – politician. BBC Newsnight 18.09.03

He was really deeply affected by some of the horrors that were happening round the world… He was aware of all these things, no doubt they also contributed to his being such a great painter. Too good for the House of Commons I tell you, too good for the House of Commons. (Talking of Robert's painting of Michael Foot).

Richard Boston – extracts from his views on the Round Room Mural given in the *Guardian*, September 1981

Twice in one week I have found my blood boiling and it wasn't the hot weather. The first time was in the peaceful village of St Germans in East Cornwall. It has a stunning Norman church which is only slightly marred by the Burne-Jones east window.

   Little did I know what was in store. Hard by the church is Port Eliot House, a stately home… architecturally, it is of no particular interest apart from the fact that it has a round room designed in 1802 by Sir John Soane.

   It is one of the most perfectly proportioned rooms that I have ever seen… the trouble is, and this is what made my blood boil, that the room has been vandalised by the abominable decorations that have recently been painted over the walls. The style is a sort of surrealist baroque in which strange

Sections of the Round Room Mural – Richard Boston fled from these, Nichola was entranced.

images tumble over one another in colours that set your teeth on edge, executed with that kind of oily finish that makes the work of Salvador Dali so very disagreeable. I registered a colossal representation of Michelangelo's David, a considerable number of portraits of the owner of the house and all sorts of peculiar goings-on which I would record if I hadn't taken steps to obliterate them from my memory.

I gave a shriek and fled. Perhaps there are people who like that kind of painting. That's a matter of taste. What can't be disputed is that these murals, hideous or not, are totally inappropriate for Soane's' delicate, airy style… all that some future owner has to do is to get a broad brush and a bucket of white paint and Soane's masterpiece will be restored to its former glory.

Nichola – a housewife who saves up to buy Lenkiewicz paintings

I now have four paintings and would like to acquire more. The first was a present from my husband, Lenkiewicz's 'Study of Lisa Stokes in a Blue Shawl'. It took a little while to get used to the size and heavy framing, even in our large Victorian room, but I admire the work greatly: the colours, the textures, the way he portrays her hair and the embroidery on the shawl. I feel I want to touch that. It gives me such pleasure.

Why do I like Lenkiewicz's paintings? It is hard to explain in a formal way as I have no training in art. It is like meeting people: there are some who you are instantly drawn to. The way 'chemistry between people' works was like that for me when I encountered Lenkiewicz paintings. There was an instant chemistry. I am fascinated by the people in his paintings. The big mural in the Barbican was my first experience. I used to go back to Plymouth just to see it. He has a way of painting that embraces the whole of humanity, a kind of naked honesty about humans that makes you accept what you see. For example, the paintings of some of his vagrants makes me see them as real people. I feel as though I almost know the person. When I study them what might elicit disgust in transient viewing shows me an almost beautiful but visceral portrait of mankind.

Earlier this year the Lenkiewicz Foundation organised a viewing of the Round Room Mural at Port Eliot which I attended. As I entered, the enormity of it immediately overwhelmed me. I turned this way and that, trying to take it all in at once but focusing only on isolated fragments, a girl's face, a silver jug showing Robert's own reflection, a Venus-like figure. After several minutes, I drew away from seeing a 'scrap book collage' and began to trace the progression of this work of art as it boldly adorned the curving wall. Commencing with the family, through death and destruction, knowledge, the joining of male and female depicted by the entwined symbolised tails of dragons. Finally there is the woodland scene, sadly unfinished, and maybe for this reason, unusually tranquil. It was entrancing.

Nichola and The Study of Lisa Stokes.

Ray Balkwill – professional landscape painter and tutor

There are two words that readily come to mind when I view a painting by Robert Lenkiewicz: 'Vitality' and 'Emotion'. His paintings are more than just literal interpretations, they also convey feelings and there is always an interaction between spirit, soul and the subject. I think this is an important ingredient in his work and probably why I enjoy the paintings so much.

His portrayal of modern day society has similarities to the great William Hogarth in his depiction of moral subjects. Although sometimes Lenkiewicz's personal reaction to his subject was shocking and controversial, they were always engaging and honest. His supreme technical skills and sensitivity with the medium was awe-inspiring, in particular his portrayal of light is reminiscent of another great portrait master, Rembrandt.

Strong praise indeed, but worthy, I believe, of an artist who was totally absorbed by his art. Painters such as Lenkiewicz do not always sit comfortably in a contemporary art world where many critics argue that 'Painting is dead!'. However, there is no doubt in my mind that his importance will reach far beyond his own time.

James Lake – graduate Fine Art (2004) Plymouth University

Technically his painting is brilliant. His handling of the paint demonstrates a rare skill, a mastery of technique that has been little seen for many hundreds of years. There is a depth and quality of colour and the near photographic quality of the brush work breathes a self contained life into the figures that inhabit his paintings.

The enduring strength and consistency of his work means that it will stand the test of time. The relevance of his work will grow, outliving the fashion or movements of the day. We will be able to return to his work in the future and find the same qualities as we see in it now.

When considering the works and this man of such brilliance I find myself asking the following question. What is wrong with this work and what is wrong with this picture? It cannot be the content of Lenkiewicz's many themes as they all have evidently been studied with passion and deep consideration. Maybe it is in the defiantly self-contained nature of the work which remains beyond the viewer. That is, there is a separation between the painter and the viewer. The paintings stand on their own and do not need the input of the viewer to complete them.

This quality of separateness and self-containment is increased further by the multiple figures crowding some of his work that only highlights the intimate nature of his single portraits, which I find more accessible. I find myself looking at these works as if looking through the veil of time, similar in experience to the act of looking at the works in the National Gallery.

'Spirit, soul and the subject' versus 'Painting is dead' (detail from Robert's The Last Supper).

Simon Butler – arts publisher

A collector friend playfully described Lenkiewicz as 'Jack Vettriano with porn', a remark in which he alluded to an element of style over substance in their respective works, a common criticism of both artists. But how can we separate the art from the artist? Is simply viewing a painting enough to make a valid judgement upon it, or are we also required to understand its creator fully to appreciate a given work?

Books such as this by Keith Nichols provide a perspective that gives a deeper understanding of the artist — and validates the publisher's role in the field of art. In simple terms, I contend, the

Vetriano with porn?

more complex the artist the more we need to know about their life in order to appreciate their work. In Lenkiewicz's case, the paintings themselves only show part of the complete picture.

Irena Boobyer – Art tutor (Open College of Arts) and President of the Exmouth Art Group

As an art tutor I have often been asked to comment on Lenkiewicz's paintings. For me they make an excellent starting point and introduction to 'what is a work of art' discussions. Lenkiewicz paints in a figurative style. If, when discussing 'a work of art' it is assumed to be a two dimensional representation of a three dimensional world then Lenkiewicz's paintings can certainly be described as such – I have heard him being described more than once as 'a modern day Rembrandt'. To widen the debate, many critics would argue that having a painting style more reminiscent of the Old Masters of the seventeenth century than twentieth century contemporaries can not be sufficient justification for calling a painting a work of art. Instead, it is the intention that informs the work that is all important. With Lenkiewicz, a discussion of his well-documented projects on Vagrancy, Jealousy, Old Age etc., give a further insight into his paintings and provide another dimension to his works as art.

Critics maintain that Lenkiewicz's most powerful works are evocatively moody, atmospheric and intense whilst his less significant works often present as quaint and chocolate-boxy. In my view, paintings by Lenkiewicz are visual reminders of a moment in time when artists with flowing locks, wearing smocks and living in abandoned warehouses were an actuality. His paintings personify the notion that artists paint because it is a way of making aspects of their world tangible and visible and he did this with extraordinary success.

Paul Overy (Alias Robert Lenkiewicz) Robert's spoof critique published in *The Times*, Wednesday 14 December 1977 under the title 'The Pilgrim Without Progress, Lenkiewicz in Plymouth'. Extracts:

For the last five years he has been working a motley series of 'Relationship' themes designed to draw attention to his 'aesthetic theory of love'. The formulae are obscure, the technique academic and the presentation kitsch.

What is particularly confusing about Lenkiewicz is his tendency to flip from page to page of his 'philosophical repertoire' in his attempt to justify the embarrassment he obviously feels in painting the way he does.

He is competent but utterly void of talent and creative force, sufficiently sophisticated to be aware of his skill and simultaneously aware of its obsolescence. He clearly has no idea what to do with himself and in this dilemma continues to paint out of sheer spite.

His theatrical notions will never be a compensation for his paucity of talent. He may paint vast mediocrities or 'themes on love' in the prodigious and hysterical manner he is used to until Antoine Wiertz rises from his grave. It will serve him and his audience nothing.

Those who purchase from him for taste are shallow, those who purchase from him for investment fools. He is of interest as proof of the cul-de-sac that superficial painting ability and talentless arrogance can drive one into. [Author's note. This was, I believe, an attack through parody on art critics in general and also stood as an ironic, inverse statement of his own self image as a painter, which he knew from daily personal experience to be robust. Great fun].

Keith Nichols – the author

Hair and mirrors have been important to Lenkiewicz. Born into a Jewish family with unusual blond hair (this possibly earning him maternal devotion), he later became a distinctive figure in Plymouth, marked by a head of long, latterly well-kept greying hair. Hair is seen to merit emphasis in many of his paintings – and he was exceptionally skilled in its portrayal. Mirrors often feature in his paintings too, partly because he had this intensity about human relationship as a mirror; that is, when we relate to others we relate only to aspects of ourselves mirrored in the other. This led to his infuriating habit of having some of his oils needlessly framed behind glass because he wanted the viewer to see his own reflection as he viewed the painting. In certain light conditions the reflection is just about all you can see, which makes the philosophical point but rather defeats the object of viewing his paintings.

David Goodwin – Webmaster, Lenkiewicz.org

Since launching the lenkiewicz.org web site in 2003, I have been asked on numerous occasions to explain my interest in Robert Lenkiewicz. Usually the person asking the question simply wants to understand what motivated me to create the site – surely I must have been a close friend of Lenkiewicz, perhaps a former student, or possibly an art lover and collector of Lenkiewicz work?

The emphasis on hair (detail from St Antony).

Invariably I struggle for a coherent and convincing answer… after all, apart from the occasional glimpse of Lenkiewicz whilst on the Barbican, or the briefest of exchanges when visiting his studio, I certainly can't lay claim to having known the man. As for my artistic talents, on a good day I would struggle to make a mediocre job of painting our spare room. Present me with a palette and canvas, and the likelihood is that you will see me beating a hasty retreat towards the nearest exit.

I must, therefore, be a lover of the arts, then? An admirer and collector of Lenkiewicz's work? Well, even a claim to this would be tenuous at best. Yes, I have a few of his limited edition prints, but probably not enough to qualify as a 'collection'. And if asked to comment on the artistic or technical merits of his work, my response would simply highlight my ignorance of the subject.

So, why the interest in Robert Lenkiewicz? I suppose that, like many Plymothians of my age, I have simply been caught in the shadow that he has cast over the city for the past three decades. Speak to any Plymothian, and they are likely to know of Robert Lenkiewicz. Furthermore, you can almost guarantee that they will have an opinion. If not on his work, most certainly on his life.

Frequently, that opinion will be supported by a very personal anecdote, presented in such a way as to suggest that it makes the speaker uniquely qualified to comment.

And now, for me, you are starting to get close to the roots of my interest in Lenkiewicz. Yes, I am an admirer of his work. Yes, I am impressed by his undoubted talents and his almost unfaltering energy for life. Yes, I have tremendous respect for the time and energy he devoted to helping others. But, at a far more fundamental level, I am simply a Plymothian.

Like others, seeing Lenkiewicz's work hanging above what seemed like every mantelpiece in the city, witnessing the creation of his murals, hearing the gossip and rumour, and reading the newspaper headlines, was all part of growing up in Plymouth. Robert Lenkiewicz simply could not be avoided!

Whether Lenkiewicz's contribution to the city was a positive one, and whether his death is a loss to the city as a whole, will no doubt divide public opinion as much as he divided it during his lifetime. However, there can be little doubt that his death has left a sizeable hole in the fabric and colour of the city.

However, to suggest that Lenkiewicz was little more than a 'local character' is clearly a tremendous disservice to the man. Others, far more qualified to comment on such things, will tell you just how great an artist Lenkiewicz was. They will highlight the importance of the sociological and philosophical thought that underpinned so much of his work. They will tell you that his paintings communicate something to the viewer about their own lives and the world they live in. They will compare this with the output of his more-lauded contemporaries, whose work seems to offer little more than fleeting eye candy.

Are they right? Well, they can certainly put together a very convincing case. Personally, if pressed to explain why I like Lenkiewicz's work, I would have to say that it is the way it forces me to have an opinion. With some notable exceptions, I find that his paintings will generally challenge me to just try and ignore them. They demand a reaction. They demand that I look, that I think, and that I learn.

I simply hope that, to some small degree, the lenkiewicz.org web site can continue the Lenkiewicz goal — for the provocation of thought.

Robert LENKIEWICZ AS A TEACHER AND PAINTER
Louise Courtnell

Author's note. As a final 'statement' concerning Robert as a painter I invited a contribution from a figurative painter who is not unreasonably described as a Lenkiewiczian. I use this phrase in the sense that she trained under Robert and although she paints in her own style it is easy to detect the lineage. Louise Courtnell knew Robert for sixteen years. Uniquely to this book she was a pupil of Robert's for five years before moving to London for a spell and then returning to the South West. Throughout this time until his death she had a contact with Robert that allowed some quite intensive tutoring experiences. In addition she was a regular sitter and, as a long time friend, came to know him very well as a person.

ROBERT AS A TEACHER

My first encounter with Robert was in 1986 when I had a studio on Plymouth's Barbican, in the New Street Gallery. I was fresh from art school and was planning an exhibition to include some portraits of local personalities. The proprietor, Francis Mallet, suggested I asked Robert to sit for me and, as I lacked the courage to ask him personally, agreed to be my 'go between'. He subsequently returned with the message that Robert would only sit for Rembrandt… but would I sit for him?

I took up the offer a week later and sat for two hours as he made an impressive first statement on a two foot by three foot canvas. I could watch the painting emerge as it was a mirror image and I remember being amazed firstly that he did no preparatory outline or drawing and, secondly, that he worked on a black canvas. The image of me just grew from blocks of colours, applied with speed and a sure hand.

Louise Courtnell.

He proceeded to tell me that he had seen my work on the Barbican, that I needed help with my dark tones and that he would teach me. I warmed to his directness and sense of colour. I really knew very little about painting as I had specialised in printmaking and, as happens these days, there is very little that is actually 'taught' at art school — one is expected to express one's thoughts and so on but the tools with which to do so remain elusive. So my apprenticeship began.

The very first painting lesson is freely etched on my mind. He had set up a white still life — a sphere, cylinder and milk bottle that was lit by a halogen lamp. It was my task, using black and white emulsion paint and a piece of black hardboard, to record the event before

Tonal Studies, Self Portrait 1988, and Cathrine Caddy 1988.

me. 'You'll make three mistakes, everyone does.' And with that he said he would return in ten minutes. I remember thinking, 'Hah. I've been to art school, mate.' And then, as I nervously mixed and dabbled, realised it was a lot harder than I'd anticipated. I awaited the clomp of his boots coming up the stairs with trepidation.

When he returned, he smiled and gave me a musical rendition of my study, which was 'God Save the Queen', very out of tune. He then sang it in tune and I realised immediately what it should have looked like. He then told me my three mistakes. They were that I had not covered all of my board, I had not mixed my greys cleanly enough and, thirdly, I had painted the shape of the objects instead of the shape of the tones. He defined tone as being, 'The lights and the darks,' and used it as the basis of his teaching which was divided into three stages: (1) the tone of the tone (2) the shape of the shape and (3) the colour of the colour.

For the next six months I was allowed to paint only in black and white and always on black hardboard, whether it was a still life in the studio or a self portrait at home (see the illustrations Catherine Caddy and Self Portrait). This gave me a basic and thorough understanding of tone. When one is interested in painting the visual world this is fundamental. It was like learning a new language which I found fascinating and challenging and I was extremely fortunate to have a very well-informed teacher who explained things clearly and concisely. I learned that the reason for using a black palette and board was that it made us mix our greys slightly darker, which made it easier to render the visual world where sometimes a light bulb, for instance, would be lighter than our white paint. Therefore, we had more control. I remember Robert saying I was like a sponge, greedily soaking up all this knowledge. In a sense, I also had to swallow my youthful pride and put myself into the hands of the master letting him see my mistakes and weaknesses.

Stage two – the shape of the shape – was to do with relating one shape of tone to another, that is, understanding the relationship between things. Part of the process is to paint the biggest shape of tone first, then the next biggest, etc. until one has covered the board. This helps us 'conceive the whole' rather than getting sidetracked with details. This is very important and is a logical, effective approach. I can hear Robert's words of advice, 'Don't get too fussy too soon.' He advised never to start a painting with a brush that was narrower than your thumb nail (I now give the same advice to my students).

I had completed a self portrait at home at this stage which I was quite impressed with and when I took it to show Robert he covered up the eyes, nose and mouth and proclaimed, 'Not a very interesting painting, is it?' After my protestations that I'd tried really hard on 'those bits', he pointed to the very bottom left hand corner of the board and said if I were to take painting seriously then every square inch should be as important as every other. This was a sobering thought. Following on from this came the most important thing that he ever taught me, 'Let every mark be a thought and every thought a clear one.' This is such good advice and I apply it still to every painting I do, which calls for a lot of concentration and tenacity.

The last stage – the colour of the colour – was the most complex. Robert talked of the saturation and dullness of colour, the tone of colour and stressed the importance of keeping colours 'fresh and clean' when mixing but he largely let me find my own way and encouraged me to read books on colour theory. He rarely gave praise but his constructive criticism was priceless and more helpful.

Having a good understanding of tone, shape and colour is relevant whether one is a figurative painter, abstract painter or private language painter. Some of Robert's students have branched off into these fields – indeed, Robert was well informed on all the different schools of art and encouraged his students to experiment and be broadminded. He saw no real distinction between them.

He often showed me works in his library by various painters, for instance, Velazquez, Rembrandt, Picasso, Matisse, Gwen John, in order to illustrate more subtle points. When I accompanied him once to London and he took me round his beloved National Gallery, his enthusiasm for painting was a joy to see. I remember him particularly praising the later 'Phillip IV' by Velazquez, and Rembrandt's 'Mrs Tripp' and the late 'Self Portrait'. He showed me how to 'drink in the colours' and examine the brush marks and the quality of the paint up close, and then walk back six feet, ten feet away, always remaining parallel to the picture plane.

My apprenticeship lasted until 1991 when I moved to London, after being commended at The National Portrait Gallery's BP Portrait Award for a self portrait. On hearing the news, Robert was sweet and encouraging. During those five years I had also modelled for Robert and had learned much from watching the maestro at work. He felt strongly that one should, 'respect the event' before one, whether it was a figure, landscape or still life. That one should be amazed by it and shouldn't compete with it. He was an unusually fast worker and moved the paint around fluidly, sometimes thin paint, sometimes thick and juicy. I used to sometimes think he treated the stuff almost adoringly. He stressed that, first and foremost, the PAINT should be interesting irrespective of the image.

ROBERT AS A PERSON

As a person, he was eccentric and extraordinary and had a huge capacity for people. I see him as someone who was brutally honest, optimistic, compassionate and magnanimous but not sentimental, having a childlike interest in and wonder at the world. He thought of his own death every morning and concluded, 'How wonderful, another day.' He also cherished his freedom.

He made me question life on moral and ethical issues and consider the hypocrisy of us all and how we make unfair demands on each other. Probably the most important thing I've learned from him as a person is to be responsible for myself and my actions. 'You're on your own'. My happiness does not rely upon another person – it is my responsibility to make my life rich and interesting and if I have relationships they are a bonus. I find this healthy and preferential.

When I first knew him, he told me that life was a tragedy, that's why we had the arts, to make it more bearable. I disagreed at the time, seeing life as a gift but I understand now what he meant: the mere fact that we are born and we die is a tragedy.

ROBERT AS A PAINTER

In a recent *Telegraph Magazine* (9 October 2004) Michael Brown referred to Robert's work as, 'One of the most singular bodies of work of any British artist of modern times.'

Robert described himself as a presenter of information on sociological issues that were common to all people. The format for this information usually consisted of hundreds of paintings on a theme, 'aesthetic notes' written by the artist and written material by sitters. The first project, 'Vagrancy', began in London in the 60s and culminated in an exhibition in Plymouth in 1973. There have been 19 projects since then, the last being 'Addictive Behaviour'. (Most of these projects have been commented on earlier in this book).

One could say that Robert was an anachronism in the contemporary art world. His style of painting was largely figurative and academic, with often very large canvases and many figures and a Rubenesque-like flamboyance. What made him a unique figure, however, was the sheer volume of work. It was his intention with all twenty projects to present a 'body of information' for each, that is, 200 plus paintings which he described as THE PAINTING. He was very unattracted to the idea of the artist intensively trying to put all his or her thoughts and feelings about something into one image – he felt there was more humility in a hundred images, produced innocently and energetically without worrying about ideas of high art.

For the Vagrancy Project he became directly involved with the lives of his sitters – drug addicts and alcoholics amongst them, after finding nine warehouses to house them all.

He said that the event of the exhibition was part of THE PAINTING and that, 'the humanities involved in putting this project together was of more importance than any art theory.' (*R.O. Lenkiewicz* – White Lane Press)

Despite this, he pushed himself technically and, from a painter's point of view, Robert's skill as a draughtsman and subtle colourist shines through in his work. In The Bishop and the Painter – Dancing to Mahler, from the Vagrancy Project, he uses a subtle combination of dull greens and violets which give a quiet and melancholic mood. It is an unusual and touching scene, a large painting (8 ft x 10 ft) where the life-size figures relate to each other in space and we feel the weight of them *(see page 95)*.

Robert worked very quickly and could feel relationships between objects, for example, head, torso and legs, with ease. He could 'conceive the whole' – sometimes imagining he was carving a figure out of wood – and never needed to sketch or check dimensions with measurements. If one doesn't paint, it is difficult to appreciate the skill involved in painting from life, especially on this scale.

For some projects, he invented his own private language and the images were often quite small scale with water-based paint on paper. They were from his imagination and experience rather than observation. A good example is The Painter with Mary, a mixed media from Project 14. It is inscribed: 'The obsessive is on, undermined by her leaving to fetch coffee, as he would be if she left to fetch Brando. The claw moves in the stomach as she leaves.' He was attempting to use the emotive qualities of colour to illustrate feelings and sensations. The figures are simplified and fluid.

It is widely known that Robert painted many self portraits. He often said that they can be one's strongest works as one is one's own best model for practical reasons. My personal favourite painting by Robert is known as Paper Crowns from Project 14. It's sometimes difficult to verbalize why a painting is great. If one stands before this painting and drinks in the colours, it is a visual feast: the most delicate of cool bluish marks above his eyebrows and on either side of her mouth; the delicious golden shadows on the paper crowns; just enough rosemadder on the nose and cheek but not too much. It is understated with dry, broad strokes (Robert often preferred square-ended brushes).

Contrary to popular understanding, it is more difficult to simplify than be near photographic with detail and it makes for a much more interesting and 'painterly' image. In my opinion, this self portrait (Paper Crowns) is a much stronger piece than, for example, the Self Portrait shown as an illustration together with Paper Crowns. The Self Portrait looks impressive and more 'finished', especially with the finely painted area of Robert's eye on the left, but for me the paint isn't as interesting and enjoyable. I am not moved by this painting as I

A painting in private language: The Painter with Mary.

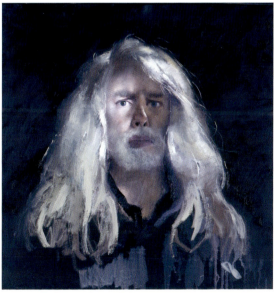

Self Portrait.

Paper Crowns.

am with Paper Crowns. There is an intimacy and a connection between the two in the latter and an air of melancholy and inevitability in their expressions. The crowns represent fools' caps – one wonders why they are wearing them. Perhaps the fragility of things, the inevitability of separation and eventual death?

Paper Crowns is a very accomplished double portrait which I would love to see hanging in the National Gallery next to a Rubens or Rembrandt; though this would be out of keeping with Robert's wish for all of the paintings in each project to be seen together as a single painting. I have not the capacity to see a hundred paintings and much prefer to 'hog' one, enjoy it selfishly and declare it a masterpiece. I think this painting equals anything by Lucian Freud, who is widely accepted as our greatest living figurative painter.

Following on from this I have sometimes lamented the fact that, especially in his latter years, Robert did not tend to spend a long time on individual paintings (I would have liked to have seen more masterpieces appear). He needed to work quickly and to produce a new image every day and, as a result, there were inevitably some weaker works. One might argue that this was detrimental to his reputation as an artist, but one also has to respect his way of working.

To the art establishment and critics, Robert's work was and is unfashionable – he has never been recognized as a serious painter. In assessing him as such, it is very important to look at his written material on 'aesthetic fascism' which relates to the human condition (therefore, every project) as well as his library collection. He saw himself as a sociological enquirer as well as a painter, and the paintings and notes have to be seen together.

I think he deserves recognition as an ambitious figurative painter who created a new genre and was in a league of his own. He was a skilled, lyrical draughtsman who took colour further than any other European painter of the last century and was possibly the most important British artist of our time.

Robert made painting his passion and made me take my work more seriously and push myself to work hard. He enabled me to see the world with new eyes, to have knowledge on the end of my brush instead of just hope. I needed this role model for me to make painting the most important thing in my life. In one sense, it has led me on a narrow, selfish and sometimes lonely journey, but for some reason applying pigment to canvas transcends me to another plane and though continuing to be hard work, is a thrilling and empowering experience.

After Robert's death Louise Courtnell painted Losing Robert, Self Portrait.

The PAINTER'S STUDIO

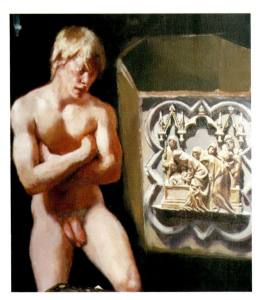

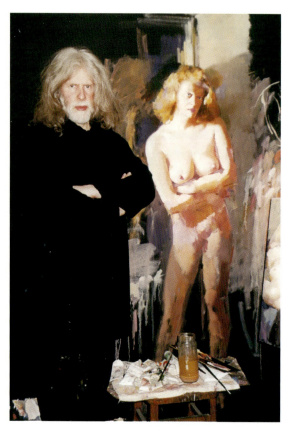
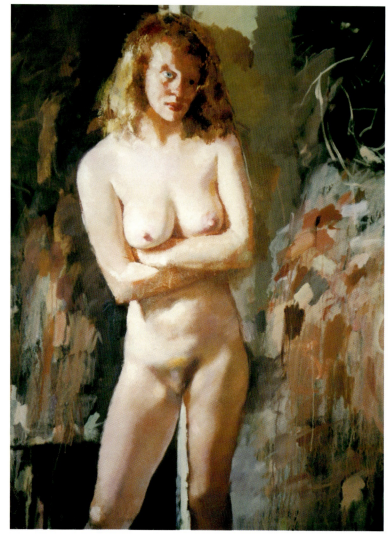

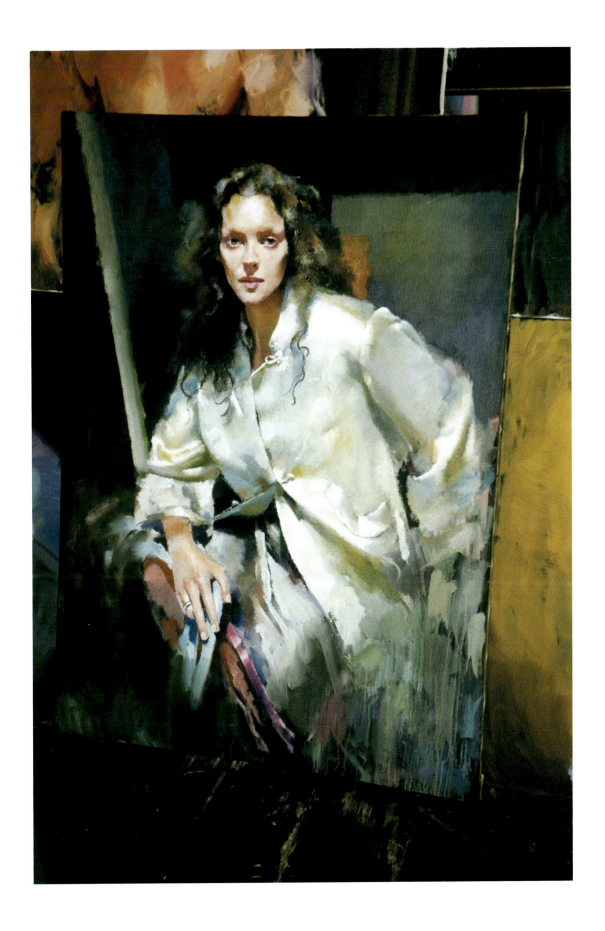

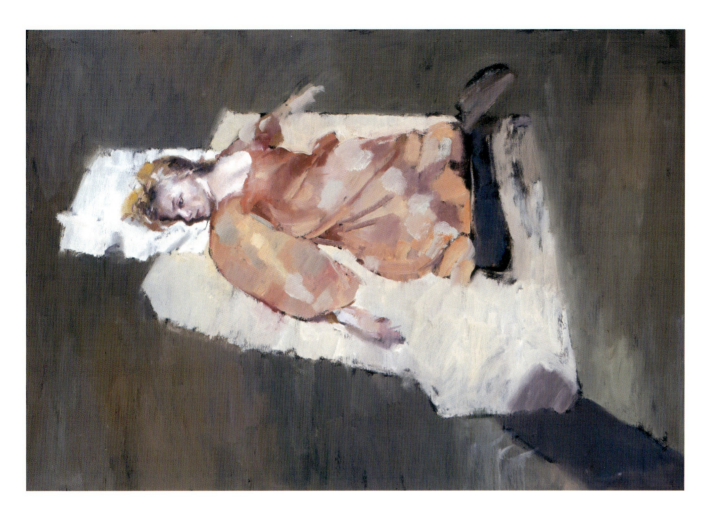

117

The EXPERIENCE OF BEING PAINTED BY LENKIEWICZ

On the occasion of my first visit to Robert at his Barbican studio, Robert ended the visit, as related above, by inviting me to sit for him. I have to be honest and say that, in the first instance, I took it as a substantial compliment. Later, though, I began to realise that, at best, it was a minimal compliment and, in reality, probably not a compliment at all. Painters need sitters and Robert got through a very great many paintings with an accordingly large number of sitters required. He also was possessed of, I suspect, a mild compulsion to ask people to sit for him for rather insubstantial reasons. In my case, I was to be a sitter for his proposed Project 20, destined to comprise 600 paintings on the theme of addiction. I did ask him to explain why he found me a relevant sitter to the theme. Robert replied that the rationale for my inclusion was because our conversations revealed that I was moderately *au fait* with certain aspects of human physiology and had revealed a sympathy with his general physiological theories in the sense that I recognised a physiological basis for certain behaviours including aesthetic attraction. Even so, I felt a little peripheral in that I did not work with addicts nor, to my knowledge, did I need therapy for any specific addiction.

Be all this as it may, it was arranged that work on the painting would start at the Barbican studio at midday on Friday 20 December 1996. This, of course, led to certain narcissistic preoccupations that needed to be solved, namely, how to dress and how to present myself (there is no point in denying that such thoughts ran through my head). Typical clothing seemed the answer to the first of these questions tempered by the fact that I had already noted that the large studio area that we were likely to be in had no meaningful heating. As for posture and context, this was not left to me since Robert already had a notion in his mind. He had said to me to bring something that was of personal significance to me and hold it for the sitting but I did not care for this idea particularly and ignored the request. Needless to say the first sitting proved a novel and instructive event:

Intense concentration before beginning the statement of the painting to be.

NOTES
Friday 20 December 1996

Arriving at the Barbican at the appointed hour, Robert got briskly to business. I was shown up a rickety ladder into a smallish gallery area that, as usual, was clut-

The statement and facial outline thirty minutes later.

tered with half finished paintings, not the least of these being a large portrait of Terry Waite. A large black canvas was already on the easel and a palette was to hand with fresh brushes and freshly squeezed daubs of paint, this preparatory work being undertaken by his personal assistant, Jane. I had somehow expected a degree of comfort but this was not to be. I ended up perched uncomfortably on a small wooden bench that, literally, had sacking on it as a substitute cushion. Next to me on a stool was an ineffectual, elderly electric fire. Robert, meantime, sat on a rather tired looking upright chair. We chatted for two minutes and negotiated a position that I thought I could hold for half an hour. He did not seem to need me to be perfectly still.

Then began the all-important task of 'statementing' the painting. Robert took a jar of oily turpentine, a palette of turpentine diluted oils and a broadish, flat brush. He peered at me very intently for a few seconds and then, with a degree of what seemed to be clear physical agitation, he made a rapid sequence of brush strokes on the canvas. This process lasted for four or five minutes and then he seemed to quieten physically a little and turned to his paints on the palette. The statementing had been a rush of creative impulse designing the portrait to be, stating the posture, the set of the body and turn of the face.

Now the painting itself began but in a quite different atmosphere. We started chatting casually as he selected colours and dealt with aspects of the upper torso and head. It was as if a plunge into a pool had been made and he could now savour the point of the plunge, that is, to be working on a near empty canvas again. The session lasted about thirty minutes and, without indicating that it had ended, Robert rose and stepped back a little, briefly to inspect his work. Then he turned away saying, 'Perhaps we might continue our conversation in the library,' so setting off down the ladder which seemed even more inadequate for his large, physical size.

We had something like six sittings at regular intervals and the portrait took form and depth. The sessions were much the same, about half an hour in length, and during these we talked on a variety of subjects. From time to time, Robert would use a mirror technique, picking up a hand mirror and inspecting the painting in reversed image. Quite often it was cold in

Yana deals with appointments while Robert paints.

A sitting in progress, note the uncomfortable bench and hopeless little electric fire.

the studio and the bench became uncomfortable after half an hour. When sittings went beyond this I did become a little restive and wondered about some of the demanding poses that his female sitters were required to adopt, lying across his lap naked for example. Did they suffer shivers and aches too?

By now, Robert's earlier personal assistant, Jane, had disappeared from the studio and was replaced by the impressive Yana Trevail. She was a longstanding friend of Robert's and had been a sitter on numerous occasions. Now, taking on a historically important role as part keeper of his appointments diary, part personal organiser and also general guardian of the studio at large, she dealt with a string of sitters and various visitors. Under her direction the sittings were well organised and I rarely waited more than a few minutes beyond the agreed time. Yana prepared things for the sitting. There were always brushes and a palette of freshly squeezed paints waiting beside the painting which would be set up in its usual place on an easel. She would telephone down to the library on the lower floor to say that I had arrived and usually painting started after a minimum of pleasantries. Yana would hover attentively, responding promptly to any call from Robert. Occasionally he would allow himself to be interrupted by a telephone call, especially in the run-up to the Retrospective exhibition in Plymouth. Yana would bring a cordless phone up the ladder for his use. He would sometimes continue to paint while he took the call.

I had fallen into the habit of arriving early, talking with Yana and wandering through the studio areas to catch up with new works. On roughly my ninth visit, I had expected another

The portrait progressing.

Conversation was often lively during a sitting.

The technique of viewing the painting through a mirror.

sitting. On this occasion, however, Yana said that Robert was not intending to paint today and would be meeting me in the library. This was fine by me and we had an agreeable three-quarters of an hour before we went out to a café for lunch together. To my surprise, the same thing happened on the next occasion, then things reverted to normal for two more visits. However, something had changed in Robert's approach and he seemed less intently involved with the painting. It was almost as if he was tinkering with it rather than trying to move it to completion. I couldn't help noticing that there were quite a lot of portraits in the studio in a similar state of completion, the face well formed with one eye complete, the upper body well depicted but the limbs and lower body trailing away into turpentine runs and broad brushed areas of colour. It felt that Robert lost interest in a painting once it reached a certain stage. I can't say that this bothered me particularly since I assumed he would finish it one day although, in fact, he never worked on it again. Instead, he started to arrange for me to meet with him in his Basement studio. In reality, this was much more exciting since it was a secret den of extraordinary productivity with a high preponderance of paintings being nude women. It was also one of his locations for sexual encounters and the preparation of the sexual notes.

Around about the year 2000, it seemed that Robert had almost ground to a halt with work on his heroic ambition to do 600 paintings for the addiction project. He was extraordinarily busy but this business was of a different kind of painting. It was rapid turnover portraits for money earning commissions required to service menacingly high levels of debt. Robert could no longer hold his dedication to non-earning projects, the sociological comments he so favoured such as the Addiction project, of which my own portrait was one of some one-hundred-and-fifty or so that had been started. When on visits a year or so after the last sitting I would climb the ladder into the studio area to check if the painting was still there. It always was, stacked with a number of other unfinished paintings. I did not take offence at this abandonment though, it did not feel like a personal thing and it was good to have had the experience of being painted by Lenkiewicz. Some have said, incidentally, that he painted me looking too young and with a little too much cranial development – but I think not, he did a good job! Curiously though, as it progressed, likeness did seem slowly to slip away from the painting.

As far as it got. My painting waits for attention alongside others.

Robert AND WOMEN

I have reflected at some length on whether or not to include this somewhat more intimate aspect of Robert's life in the book. I had to conclude that women were such a large part of his life, his painting, his notes, his behaviour and his thinking that it would be a major distortion to avoid the issue. The fact that there would be any hesitation would, in itself, amuse Robert.

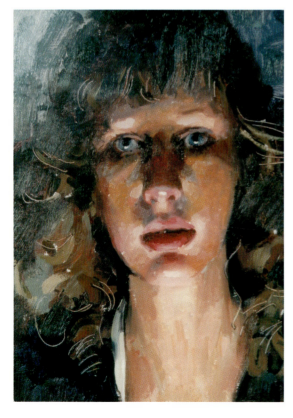

There is something of an ever-present injustice in the caprice of human interest. It is a regular experience that, when in conversation and it comes to light that I knew Robert, people will often say, 'Oh yes, he is the one with all the women and the dead tramp'. His recognition as one of our greatest painters is sometimes eclipsed by the reputation earned by his adventures involving the media and the general word concerning his 'womanising'. The latter comes, in part, from Robert's quite public claims to have initiated three thousand sexually-based relationships. This claim was repeated in the *Telegraph Magazine* as recently as October 2004. As I have made clear earlier, I have always been a little sceptical about the overall numbers but there is no doubt that there is a genuine basis for the claim, even if scaled down somewhat, that Robert achieved a staggering number of relationships with women when compared with the norms in our society. Incidentally, readers should be alerted to the fact that, on occasions, Robert referred to his sexual partners as 'aesthetic packages'.

Having drawn attention to 'the reputation', my conversations with Robert led me to the view that it was his calculated intent to promote this notoriety because he sought publicly to live out an ideal that he held dear, an ideal that was acted out through the medium of multiple relationships. In Project 8 there is a small watercolour sketch of a sexual encounter and with it some notes that serve to illustrate this rationale for his sexual history:

> *Your infidelity is not in sleeping with my best friend, my brother, my son, a stranger, but in sleeping with me. I am not the same person in any given moment let alone in the reflection of your taste extension. Faithlessness is implicit in your faithfulness. Your exclusive attention is necessarily faithless.*
> *Your exclusiveness excludes me. My exclusiveness excludes you.*

And thus:

> *Be faithful to me by feeding your attractions in all directions — you will be the richer for me.*

This was Robert's charter for multiple sexual relations, a general call for the end of monogamy and faithfulness in relationships. It flew the flag of his opposition to 'aesthetic fascism', illustrating his point that possessiveness amounts to treating people as property which in turn leads on to destructive tensions and jealousy. In principle he loathed possessiveness although, as I have remarked earlier, in practice he depended on it and selectively encouraged it. There are also elements of his personal history that conflict with his ideal. He had married three times although apparently rationalised these marriages by saying that they were for 'practical purposes'. Early extended relationships such as that with 'Mouse' and the long pursuit of Mary (in which, according to *The Mary Notebook* Robert fell victim to his own emotional mechanisms and became possessive and jealous) demonstrate that he did, in fact, relate long term. Of most note, perhaps, is the finding that, as I got to know him, the same female figures in his life kept recurring, some in a stable role equivalent to that of quasi partner, some as long-term lovers and some in a stable supporting role as close associates. The pattern of these stable relationships did not appear to change in the six years of my contact with Robert, *it was always the same women — he clearly did make and retain stable relationships*. However, with this resource of stable relationships as a platform from which to operate, Robert lived out his notion of transitory sexual relationships with a very large number of women, creating new relationships even, it would seem, in the last year of his life.

Robert talked fairly openly to me concerning his sexual partners and activities and failed, in many respects, to maintain the confidentiality that most of them would have wanted. While I can see no reason to be evasive about the sexual side of Robert's life, since it was quite public, at the same time I feel that the secrets he shared that truly belonged to others should stay protected. So I intend only to establish a general picture of this side of his life without any issues of identity arising. He indicated to me that many of his sexual partners were women who also served as sitters, although I should say that I do not know what proportion of his population of sitters were sexually involved with him. Certainly not all, since I have met sitters who declined sexual contact with him. *There is, thus, no inevitability that a sitter was a sexual partner.*

When we talked of his sexual activity, which was quite often, Robert's account would vary according to his mood. If feeling flippant he sometimes trivialised it calling himself 'sexoholic'. When more serious he called up another explanation explaining that, at the heart of this apparent sexual profligacy, there was a long-term research project. The records of this research were the so-called 'aesthetic notes'. These notes tended to be large volumes each with the title of a particular female partner. Robert would ask his partners to record an encounter with written notes accompanied by simple watercolours. He was especially interested in colour as a representation of visceral feeling. In the book *R.O. Lenkiewicz* Robert gives a clear history on the origin of this project. In his four year pursuit of Mary he fascinated himself by keeping copious notes on his personal and bodily feelings provoked by her rather tardy sexual reaction to him. This he clearly experienced as a motivating form of rejection that further invigorated the chase. He illustrated these feelings in terms of colour embedded in or emanating from the figures of himself or the 'aesthetic package' (in this case Mary). It was a study aimed at proving the point that the immediate response to someone that 'we fancy' is a simple, addicting, physiological reaction. After this episode he recounts how he realised that it made more sense and generated richer material to have the continual procession of sexual partners make their own notes and watercolours, always with an emphasis on the depiction of visceral feeling by colour.

Was this sexual psychopathy? At one level the answer has to be yes in the sense that the majority of couplings will have been in the absence of much depth of feeling on Robert's part - often construed by him as a form of research. In contrast it was (one assumes) the often strong feelings evoked in his female partners that provided the focus of this research. Of this body of material, the 'aesthetic notes' that is, Robert wrote 'nobody must see it or make observations about it, whether they are well disposed or indifferent, until I'm dead.' He did not keep to this principle with that much devotion however, since, on occasions he would illustrate a point in conversation with me by withdrawing a volume of 'aesthetic notes' and showing it to me. On one occasion he offered a degree of access to some notes for me to browse through. These books of notes, letters and personal illustrations have now been removed and secured by Robert's executor. Hopefully at some point in the future some of Robert's sexual partners will feel able to tell their story. Meantime transcript taken from various conversations that I had with Robert allow glimpses into this side of his life.

Having viewed examples of illustrations in various aesthetic notes it seems appropriate that the general nature of these should be conveyed. I have called upon the assistance of local artist Sally Moore, to recreate a typical entry as a composite from photographs. She has kindly generated a watercolour that faithfully replicates the simple nature of the illustrations, with the emphasis on colour to represent body sensation. Robert's own early products can be seen in The Mary Notebook.

NOTES

13 November 1998

KN: 'How do your current interpersonal involvements stand at the moment?'
RL: 'There are forty-seven ongoing erotic relationships in all.' [Author's note: inquiries elsewhere suggest that some of these contacts would involve one contact during a year and although the overall number might be a high estimate it was not out of all proportion].

25 July 1999
KN: 'You look tired Robert.'
RL: 'Yes I am, but things are going well, yesterday I had seven sittings and four sets of 'aesthetic notes' were made.'

KN: 'That implies that you had sexual encounters with four separate women yesterday, is that so? How do you keep going?'

RL: 'Yes, that is so. But today I am less active and will spend tonight alone working through the night to finish a painting. If I tire I will rest on the bed – but not sleep.'

24 November 1999

KN: 'Are you still as active interpersonally?'

RL: 'I would say yes, I believe that there are thirty-four ongoing contributors to the 'aesthetic notes'. I find that sexual repleteness allows one to work more intensively.'

KN: 'How are the energy levels?'

RL: 'At times I feel knackered. I would prefer not to have sex with a third or more of them – if I did not feel obliged to that is. I can't tell you what a chore it is at times.'

KN: 'Why all the relentless sex then, when will enough be enough?'

RL: 'It is for The Notes. I must continue until I have enough evidence.'

KN: 'Evidence in what sense? What is the basic research question?'

RL: 'To show that all moral and ethical judgements are formed as aesthetic experiences – this physiological sense of pleasure is 'the good'.

KN: 'How do you react to the charge that it damages the women involved, that they become addicted to relations with you?'

RL: 'Their pain is their pleasure. Darker judgements like 'it's wrong' and 'do not do this', are also aesthetically pleasurable. As in fanaticism.'

KN: 'You do not worry about any of your partners?'

RL: 'I'm squeamish about upsetting or hurting one or two but I will not concede one altruistic cell in my body.' [Author's note: in fact this was delusion. It seems that Robert was sufficiently concerned for and generous to some of his women friends that it added to his financial distress, furthermore at other times he named one or two that he was very fond of and strongly wanted to avoid wounding].

11 December 2000

RL: 'My thesis is that attraction to ideas is a physiologically based addiction, as in religious fanaticism, anti-Semitism and so on. I use sexual attraction as an investigatory tool – sexual tastes are similar physiological processes. I use myself as a guinea pig so that records can be obtained of the woman's physiological experiences.'

KN: 'And do you have a sense of an overall finding?'

'Come in – I can't be threatened by shadows in the dark.'

RL: 'I look for patterns. The differences are fewer than the similarities.'
KN: 'Are you able to talk me through some of the patterns?'
RL: 'The evidence speaks for itself through the notes.' [Author's note: Robert would not be pushed further. If there were findings of substance he did not want to discuss them].
KN: 'Two questions. How many sets of notes are there, and do you have a sense of how many women may be in love with you at the present time?'
RL: 'There are three thousand sets of 'aesthetic notes'. As to the other matter I would say between forty and forty-five – that is, they think they are in love with me.' [Author's note: In the book *R.O. Lenkiewicz* (1997) he talks of several hundred sets of notes, not three thousand, it is unclear whether all sexual partners generated notes].

14 February 2002

KN: 'But do you take pleasure in the endless sexual encounters for The Notes?'
RL: ' Of course, most of the time great pleasure. My pleasure comes from their pleasure. Sex is a metaphor, I am not in love with the person. Sex brings the rare aesthetic qualities of a woman into focus. I like to play them like a fine instrument. Then I get lost in them. It tells Self to fuck off – Self disappears. If I go down on them and get it right I disappear. I can be very moved. It turns the relationship into a muse. It can get misty and inspiring.'

Examples of written entries within the 'aesthetic notes' left me feeling that Robert was kidding himself if he thought that all his partners dealt with this arrangement in a phlegmatic manner. Some of the notes that I have seen revealed quite tortured feelings – anger, extreme possessive needs, jealousy and even panic at not being able to meet with Robert more regularly and to possess him personally. On the other hand I have met and talked with some women who managed to deal with the problem of possessiveness with some elegance and so maintained a rewarding long-term relationship with Robert, accepting that it was a very different type relationship but, even so, something of a privilege. They were at peace with it.

An interesting and somewhat different perspective on dealing with the unconventional sort of relationship that Robert offered came from conversations with a long-term female friend and sexual partner of his who first began a relationship with Robert in the late seventies. This continued for many years. She described the atmosphere between them as that of respectful friends. The relationship had an on and off pattern through the years but was comfortable as a relaxed relationship, each respecting boundaries and working to avoid being controlling. This settled stability seemed to depend on an adaptive approach in the sense of, 'I realised that I was not a key relationship and adopted a "take him or leave him" attitude from the start. It was more about having fun.'

Further observations by her offer other useful insights. Robert, she believed, disliked being attracted to individual women because it distracted him and he felt he lost power, especially, it seems in Mary's case. His habit of continually making new relationships was a way he adopted of dissipating the problem. Linked to this, I learned, Robert was not a stereotypical sexual hunter. He avoided making an overt first move but manipulated women into taking the initiative. He would offer an intense and flattering interest, the seductive thrill of being painted, possibly nude, and a well rehearsed sequence of penetrating questions and comments. The pathway to the bed (there was one in every studio) was clear and inviting yet made to feel secure by a favourite phrase of his, 'The only time this relationship will end is when one of us dies.' But the initiative tended to lie with the woman involved.

As is apparent in the transcript above, in later years the notion of sex being a chore began to creep in. This was something that my contact had also noted: 'Sometimes he felt he just had to do it but didn't really want to. Some women came for the sex. Often the sex was just curiosity because he didn't fancy them and once was enough. But he couldn't bring himself to say this to them. Later on he even told some that he was impotent – although he wasn't if he did fancy them.'

I have to bear in mind that I knew Robert when he was fading physically and needing to resort to the adaptations of the older, not very well, male. Hence an increasing emphasis on oral sex. In January 1999 he commented:

> RL: 'I have fifteen erotic relations a week – they pass one another on the stairs. But I only have full intercourse with two of them, otherwise I go down on them. They complain, some of them are very unhappy about it but I just prefer it that way.'

Most studios included a bed as essential furnishing.

Robert did report growing fatigue if he was a little low. In December 2000 he announced that he was 'on the slide, my kidney function is weakening'. He followed this with a story of being 'jumped on' by a sitter and having to tell her, 'I'm old, tired and ill.' In February 2002 he made the comment, 'I'm very jaded – in everything.' This followed a difficult week when, he related, an instance of possessiveness had turned into a stalking problem that apparently came to a rather frightening head. At the same time there was no giving up in his relentless quest for sexual linkage with women. As late on as spring 2002 Robert was talking to myself and others of new involvements and a tentative plan to provide accommodation for a woman friend of his.

How to resolve all this? Robert was passionately interested in and devoted to women and certainly meant them no harm. They filled much of his life and thoughts. I commented earlier that, as his behaviour demonstrated, he had great fidelity to *women* rather than to any one specific woman – an approach that seems inherently harmful to a significant proportion of women. At the same time he created a more personal world where there *were* stable relationships with women who provided the basis for his artistic, domestic, commercial and organisational viability. To the onlooker it appeared that there was an element of self sacrifice in these women. Some clearly loved him and gave much time to him in devoted attention and service. Otherwise he did not seem to want or require the presence of individual women for more than two hours at a time but he did want the resource of women within beckoning distance. If he is to be believed some three thousand women tolerated this arrangement to one degree or another. Quite why is an issue for speculation now and research later. Part of it has to be that Robert was very different, very charismatic, very powerful, very cultured, very intellectual and very talented. He also appeared to understand what women found attractive in the same way that he understood painting. He was a physically attractive man with a fine, handsome face and large build who must have held an unusual promise of sexual satisfaction and adventure. Curiously though, he was not, in later years at least, proud of his physical self and preferred, I have been told, to remain partially clothed during sex. Also, it seems, he did have spectacles that he kept very private and hidden.

Robert was clearly an immediately compelling presence to a large proportion of the women that he met. I rather like the story told to me by Sally Moore in recalling an incident some years ago. As a mature student at Plymouth art college she had not met Lenkiewicz but was aware of him and had basically taken a dislike to him because of his reputation as a sexual predator. At an open day event at the college Robert unexpectedly swept through the room in which she was working and, quote 'There was a kind of "oooh" feeling and I definitely went weak at the knees. He had such presence, charisma and sexual magnetism.' She also recalled that, some years later, two middle-aged women from her art group visited the Barbican studio and came across Robert painting. They returned, she reports, all 'fluttery'. One might say that Lenkiewicz was a modern day Raphael. He would have been well aware of that particular role model's propensity for 'womanising'. Robert even dressed Raphaelesque for the part.

Musing on the origins and maintenance of the behaviour it has to be kept in mind that Robert's initiation to and disinhibition with sex began early in life in his parents' hotel. He tells of mild sexual encounters with the maids from as early as eleven and involvement in intercourse at fourteen. His own explanations for his profligacy range from indications that it was all the conscious act of a consumer: 'We are always being attracted to people but most of us keep these

Charisma and sexual magnetism?

attractions as fantasies. I just put them into action,' through to the intellectually driven crusade to demolish aesthetic fascism. Here, he had the dramatic concept of himself in a guinea-pig role to provide a basis from which women might generate 'aesthetic notes' and provide evidence for the theory of the physiologically addicting basis of interpersonal attraction, religious belief, fanaticism and, I suppose, everything . Added to all this Robert must, frankly, have been blessed with a high level of testosterone that combined with an addiction prone disposition. In short, he was addicted to sex and built a fabric of rationalisation around the behaviour. His paintings of women sometimes seem to suggest a theme of sexual possession that conflicts with his 'people are not property' stance. This might be construed as a public statement with a competitive edge – it is not clear. Another issue is that painters need sitters and a prolific painter needs an endless queue of sitters. The attraction of a relationship with a great man may well have secured a large amount of sitter time.

It seemed to me that Robert took some self-confirmation in his talent at sex and also that he enjoyed a sense of rivalrous supremacy in the sheer numbers involved. In other words it was a competitive 'male thing'. It is difficult not to view the claim that he made to myself and others that in one extended encounter he induced a total of fifty-four orgasms in a partner as anything other than triumphal competitiveness.

The question arises as to whether Robert felt any guilt towards the women in his life. There were occasional glimpses that guilt did trouble him in the sense that he was mindful of misgivings and a sense of betrayal. This was conveyed to me in a conversation that I see as the most poignant and revealing that Robert and I ever had:

Some paintings may be intended to hint at sexual possession.

NOTES
Friday 7 December 2001
The Study at Castle Dyke Studio

KN: 'There is an obvious Christian theme in your painting at present – The Last Supper and The Crucifixion, which is curious. But I am most curious that you use yourself as the sitter for Judas Iscariot. Is there a personal statement involved, is it something to do with Jewish issues?'

RL: 'Judas has always fascinated me. He is cast as the eternal scapegoat but he was probably a practical zealot. It is likely that he saw Jesus as a means of provoking an uprising for a political cause and was prepared to be used this way. There was a curious tension between Jesus and Judas. Judas was, in a sense, sexy. I am not saying that he was homosexual. I have often speculated on the frame of mind he was in – to betray the son of God - almost equivalent to the devil. I put myself in Judas's place because **I am a kind of betrayer – I betray women and I betray art.**'

The 'statement' of Robert's image to portray Judas Iscariot, The Betrayer.

The betrayal of women in Robert's life was obvious, when viewed in conventional terms. The betrayal of art less so. It was a sad moment. It suggested that Robert experienced an occasional recognition of his manic behaviour pattern, his need for scale and number and the kaleidoscope of endless new relationships and saw how these bled away the potential within him for epic works of art.

I am struck by the comparison between Robert and another contemporary figurative painter, Frank Auerbach. This rather haunted man has laboured at length with his paintings, sometimes taking up to two years on some. He has worked 364 days a year with just a handful of sitters who have sat for him at regular times each week for between ten and forty-two years. If Robert had resolved the issues that drove him at such a pace and led to such continuing over-inclusiveness in relationships he may have moved on to a more reflective period of contained work and we would be even richer in art works for it.

Once in a while someone says to me, 'Come on, be honest, what did you really think and feel about Robert and all the women?' I cannot avoid the question. I think that Robert was, in the broadest sense of the word, more faithful than he would like to have generally known:

24 November 1999

KN: 'Are you saying that you place no value on long-term relationships and that there is no place for them in your life? If so it is a bit confusing to see you relating to women who have obviously been around for quite a few years.'

> RL: 'No, that is not my case. I am perfectly capable of long-term relationships. There are several that have lasted in excess of thirty years.'

In contrast to this confession a favourite public statement of Robert's was that, *'If one had genuine concern for one's partner the first thing one would do is leave them.'* He made the similar point that to inflict oneself on anyone for any length of time was a cruelty. As observed before, Robert did not live out this creed with any real conviction. In fact, he maintained a host of long-term relationships although, it has to be noted, none of them as exclusive relationships.

It is clear that from an early age Robert was intensely attracted to women and became addicted not just to sexual encounter but also to the thrill of the first sexual encounter with a new partner. He was an addictive personality. Thus, having discovered his remarkable attractiveness to women, he drifted into a situation where he had the loyal and *tolerant* support of a core of long-term partners and associates which gave him the freedom to develop the habit of endlessly beginning new relationships. They indulged him and he exploited the indulgence. The thing about 'research' into the process of physiological addiction in aesthetic attraction has never struck me as having that much substance, I regard it more as a sophisticated rationalisation, although it is entertaining enough. It will not, like some of the great bodies of thought and research, bring about change in our culture though. Having said this, some of his key points, 'people are not property etc.' are salutary and thought provoking reminders. Added to which, some of the 'aesthetic notes' are probably minor works of art in their own right. Overall, though, if pressed to fall on one side or the other I have to say that my view is that Robert was evasive about his 'findings' in the 'aesthetic notes' because little of import (in terms of advancing knowledge) will be found recorded in the notes. The whole thing was a fabric of rationalisations that gave him a lifelong licence for a never-ending stream of sexual relations. He may well have convinced himself with the rationalisations but even that I doubt, judging from his evasiveness on the issue.

I also have to point out a confusion in Robert's thinking. He likes to try to convince us that struggling to achieve fidelity is physiologically impossible because of the continual process of replacement of cells and molecular structure in our body. In physical composition, specifically, we are different people every few weeks or so it is true. Therefore, Robert argues, effectively we relate and make love to different people when we couple with our partner over the months and are therefore inherently unfaithful. This is flimsy nonsense, of course. What we know as the other person is their 'design' and the 'programme' that they are running on – the body shape and characteristic movements, facial expressions, the quality of the voice, the atmosphere of the personality, the kindness or harshness, the way of tossing the head, the way of greeting, etc. These are relative constants. Although the material substance of the body may indeed be continually changed through life, the design and system that uses these materials does not change much. As a rationale for infidelity it will not do at all.

These are some of my thoughts but what do I *feel* about Robert and women? There is regret for the 'casualties', admiration for the boldness and scale of the endeavour and, since it might be said that he had the extravagant best of both worlds, it is difficult not to feel envy. At one level I feel refreshed by the honesty of his position in that he lived out, virtually guilt free, what most men know and most women do not want to know. Namely, that the 'system design' of the average male means that they make love to a body as much as to a person. Since one body is much the same as another substituting one for another is a built in capability and therefore quite easy, were it not for an overlay of female inspired guilt. Many men could and would live like Robert if they were not held back by guilt. Set against this it can be a fine experience to immerse oneself in an intense friendship with a woman and wake up each morning to find yourself next to your best friend in life. As always with Lenkiewicz there is ambivalence.

Robert was preoccupied with the St Antony theme.

Robert's preoccupation with the St Antony theme (the monk in the desert tempted by devils) suggests that he was aware of the 'double bind' message of women in our society. Sometimes he likened women to devils that plagued him with distraction and temptation picking up the issue, perhaps, that a significant proportion of women maintain a constant effort at sexually attracting men yet punish them for responding. In some ways his sexual history can be seen as a way of confronting and subduing this type of dominance. In the following section I will consider Robert's relationship with his mother and whether that may have influenced his basic stance towards women.

I am sensitive to the certainty that feminist activists will strongly disapprove of me for having given a neutral and possibly tolerant account rather than a clearly critical assessment of the Lenkiewicz stance toward women. That's as may be. But I do have to say to him, 'Frankly, Robert, if you can hear dear friend, you would have helped the basic position a little if you hadn't pushed it and kept referring to women as aesthetic packages.'

ROBERT AS A PARENT

After some deliberation I have decided to leave this issue alone. Robert had eleven children and I have worried that the act of inquiry would be intrusive for them and felt that representing all of the different experiences would be problematic. Suffice it to say that, although Robert made public some controversial views on parenthood, not the least being the belief that children did not need their father until their 'teens', at times in private conversation he came close to being an admiring father and seemed to have a good affection for his children.

Robert with a 'devil' of sexual temptation.

Towards AN UNDERSTANDING

The point has now been reached where some effort at an analysis is called for. To restate the position; while it is true that I am a practising clinical psychologist it is not the case that I was working with Robert in some kind of therapy or professional capacity. Our relationship was essentially that of a friendship that allowed a type of enduring inquiry and observation. Robert was fully aware of this, of the intended book and of the appraisal by a psychologist. He may, of course, have played up to this particular audience.

CREATIVITY AND 'THE MID-LIFE CRISIS'

One of the things that attracted me to Lenkiewicz in the first place was the immediate impression of his quite remarkable productivity and work drive. This was not just an idle comparison with my less-motivated self but there was also an element of professional interest. For some years I had been rather taken with a theory put forward by Elliott Jacques, a psychoanalyst. Writing to the title 'Death and the Mid-Life Crisis' (*International Journal of Psychoanalysis*, 1960, Vol. 41) Jacques describes his interest in highly creative people. He had conducted a survey into the biographies of 310 past figures of known great creative stature – authors, painters, composers and so on. This led to an unexpected observation, namely, that around the middle years of this group a much higher proportion of them died than was predicted by normal death rates. He cites Mozart, Raphael, Chopin and Baudelaire as part of the large group. Linked to this Jacques made a second observation. He noted that, prior to the middle years of highly creative people, their style of creativity tended to be of an uninhibited, unrelenting outpouring of creative works, one tumbling after another almost before the former was finished. This phase of creativity Jacques labelled 'precipitate creativity' although, personally, I am inclined to call it the phase of torrential creativity for the obvious reason that the creativity was in the form of a torrent. Following this, during the period after the middle years, Jacques noted that the creative style tended to change to a much more reflective, paced approach, often with a more tragic, philosophical theme. The pressure of productivity fades and there is a greater concern on the part of the artist or composer to refine a particular work to a point of perfection. This, he called, the 'sculpted phase' of creativity.

Unexpectedly, perhaps, this article is the origin of the popular phrase, 'the mid-life crisis'

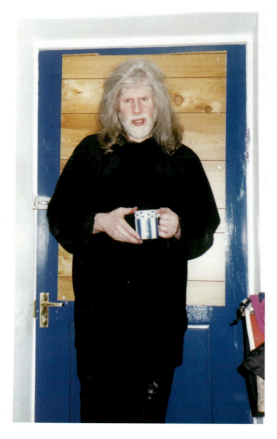

which, sadly, has been corrupted into mindless tabloid use. Jacques used it specifically in relation to highly creative people. His key point was that, in early years, creative people, in common with most young people, have a sense of a future stretching on unbounded by any end point. It is a form of denial of mortality. The highly creative, he argues, have a sense of an enormous volume of work to complete with yet more ideas crowding the earlier ones for space. No recognition of mortality or the limits of lifespan is admitted but, instead, there is a continuous profusion of work that, Jaques believes, is a manic defence against the recognition of mortality and the truth of limited lifespan. This denial cannot last and eventually, usually in the middle years, the death of someone close or the onset of personal illness breaks the denial and the truths of personal mortality have to be faced. With this comes the realisation that the plans and ambitions driven by intense creative urges cannot all be achieved and there tends to follow collapse in morale and often depression with the recognition 'that all cannot be accomplished'. Sometimes the depression can stop creative people in their tracks. Michelangelo produced little in a creative lull between the ages of forty and fifty-five, for example. *This is the event that Jacques termed the 'mid-life crisis' because, he believed, the crisis of depression could stifle creativity and lead on to premature death through physical decline.* The creative people who successfully work through the crisis tend, then, to accept the limitations of lifespan and settle for what can be achieved. Hence the change of emphasis into the slower, more refined, sculpted creativity with its emphasis on a more tragic, philosophical content that may eventually move on to the serenity of acceptance.

I find this an elegant and rather intriguing theory that holds an aesthetic appeal in itself. After my first look around the Barbican studio with its overwhelming impact of torrential creativity, I felt immediately that Lenkiewicz might be an important discovery as a living case example. If anything shouted 'manic defences' to me it was the first walk through the vast array of paintings in the Barbican studio – the productivity was manic in the strict sense of the word. Lenkiewicz was in a perpetual sprint, no measured pace of the marathon runner or the sense of a person in 'sculpted' creative mode. As I related earlier, it felt important to question Robert on the issues, hence our first meeting. I asked him if he felt he had experienced such a crisis and if his creative style had changed. He gave me a definite 'no' to both of these and said that, at the age of fifty-four at the time, if anything, his pace was accelerating and he was approaching some kind of peak of productivity. Although he did concede that his high productivity was driven by debt and that as he had matured he had become more absorbed in 'the musical quality of paint itself.' It was something of a let down but then various other issues emerged that led me to see that Jaques was unlikely to be of central relevance in understanding Lenkiewicz. One aspect of his personal history to be noted was that denial of mortality as a major factor seemed unlikely in the sense that Robert's upbringing in the Hotel Shemtov led to an early and repeated exposure to ageing, illness and death. Then his father died relatively early in Robert's life. He reveals a preoccupation with death rather than a denial and has painted and written on the theme for years.

A CORONARY PRONE PERSONALITY?

A second aspect that took the focus of my attention away from the theory of Mid-Life Crisis was my acquaintance with the news of a much more recent event. In 1992 Robert had run up against cardiac problems that led to tiredness and breathlessness, the early signs of coronary heart disease. Attention from the cardiologists resolved things for a while but Robert's heart was struggling. Eventually, in 1995, a quintuple coronary bypass was required. People only have this surgery if they have coronary artery disease, that is, the slow reduction in flow capacity of the arteries supplying the heart because the vessels are slowly being blocked by fatty deposits. Here was a second curious coincidence for me since, being a clinical psychologist who worked sessions for a cardiac department, this opened the door to an entirely different explanation for Robert's exceptional productivity, an explanation from my everyday world of work. In short, as I got to know him it became more obvious that elements of Robert's behaviour were typical of the coronary prone personality and behaviour pattern.

If I may take one paragraph to elaborate this concept I believe that readers will see the relevance. While the primary risk factor for coronary heart disease is probably genetic, other factors such as smoking and lifestyle add to the risk significantly. The standard description of the coronary prone personality and behaviour pattern is summarised as:

- an exceptional workload, multiple demands and deadlines
- heavily extended work hours
- intensive involvement
- competitive needs
- minimal rest, leisure, holidays
- chronic physical exhaustion (may be masked)
- rejection of self-care
- denial of risk

Combined with a smoking habit and lack of exercise this profile raises the risk of heart problems considerably. Robert neither drank nor smoked but the other elements in this stereotype certainly do bring the name Lenkiewicz to mind. He suffered coronary heart disease such that, in the last year or so, if he and I walked together the short distance from the Tudor Rose tea rooms to the new studio his pace was slow and he was quite breathless. This was clearly someone with a serious decline in cardio-respiratory function. In his last year a problem of cardiac arrhythmia complicated things further. *Yet*, right up until the last, Robert was an incredibly driven man often denying himself sufficient sleep, rarely taking rest or holidays and refusing to pay much attention to his declining health. His life was meticulously scheduled with hour-by-hour appointments, sitters and personal arrangements all entered into the large diary that he always carried with him. He rejected self-care, choosing

Robert in 1998 with his ever present diary/note book.

to see his intensely-driven lifestyle, that he knew was risky, as something that he could 'get away with'.

Early on in my relationship with him I did make an effort to add to the nagging of the 'concerned'. In an incident that, in retrospect, was comic, Robert, Anna Navas, Esther Dallaway and I assembled by arrangement in his office/library in the Barbican studio one afternoon in 1996. Robert sat on his lovely carved library chair, the two women on the floor and me on a stool. I gave a short tutorial on the link between coronary heart disease and lifestyle and the problem of exhaustion so urging him to reform, slow down, take more rest. Robert listened politely while Anna and Esther nodded strong agreement. Having finished my offering Robert smiled a tolerant acknowledgement, made little comment, somehow signalled that the women should leave and we carried on talking about other things as if nothing had been said. His rejection of the warnings was inevitable because, in my experience, that is how it always is with the coronary prone personality – until the heart attack occurs that is. Robert did not actually have a heart attack but he had enough health scares to acquaint him with the risks. Even so the pace was unrelenting and his attitude uncompromising:

NOTES
September 1999 St Saviours

KN: 'After your bypass and these ups and downs in health what are your thoughts about illness and death?'
RL: 'I have always had a fascination with death. It does not trouble me. I find death exhilarating, I regard it as sweet oblivion. At one point they said I could have been dead within two days without treatment. After the surgery I gave myself five years. I have always had this feeling of being about to die.'
KN: 'Have you slowed down to conserve your health at all?'
RL: 'Quite the opposite. Since I became ill I have increased my work. I fight tiredness or 'flu – I cannot find it acceptable. I now work 9.00am to 9.00pm with continual sittings. Sometimes I work at night. Ever since I was seven years old I have felt a sense of quest. I have always felt this and it is stronger now. My life work is coming to a crescendo, demand is increasing. I feel the sense of urgent quest to bring things together in completion.'

It would, frankly, be hard to find a more conforming example of a coronary prone behaviour pattern than this. It provokes a dilemma though. In his driven way he crammed so much into his sixty-one years. At the same time he probably threw away twenty years by bringing forward in time the onset of his cardiac problems. A slower, less manic Robert might have achieved some of his great dreams, not the least of which was that of his 'Sistine Chapel

Ceiling'. I ask readers to look at the three adjacent photographs. They are some my most favourite revealing a man indeed driven by a relentless quest. We were in the St Saviours building in July 1999, sitting talking about Robert's nearly completed deal to secure the new studio building. He elaborated some of his plans for the building including a plan to create a decorated roof. It was to be his Michelangelo piece, a Sistine Chapel style ceiling in the heart of Plymouth. Robert reached out for a book and drew out from its cover a sketch of the ceiling as he envisaged it. The photographs tell the story. This was a virtuoso rendition of the coronary prone personality aria. You can see the strain and fatigue on Robert's face. He is slowly fading with heart failure yet as he senses himself weakening he quickens the pace and strives harder. Now, his quest has a *long-term* focus. A plan for a painted ceiling and mural that will be the pride of Plymouth and, no doubt, a rebuttal to the 'London mob'. The fantasy was of just a few years up and down scaffolding, lying flat at times to paint (which he could not readily do because of the fluid in his lungs from the heart failure).

Did Robert really believe that he only had five years to live as far back as 1995 or, in reality, was it brave talk that he did not really believe? With a plan like this he could not, in his heart, believe that his death was around the corner. There had been talk of a heart transplant and since his friend Perry Eliot had survived another form of transplant surgery there was hope in the air. It was not unreasonable hope either – if only he would have relented a little and given his body a chance. The problem was (to allow myself a moment of theatre that Robert would very much approve of) that the bell was tolling but he would not let himself hear it.

A comment on one of the other features in the list above, competitiveness. Was Robert competitive? Yes, in various ways, is the answer that comes to my mind. In earlier days, according to Lord St Germans, he was very competitive physically. He would take delight in lifting heavier weights than others around him, such as gravestones. He could also be

Robert with his sketch of his Sistine Chapel to be – note the tiredness in his face.

Detail of the ceiling cartoon.

Part of the loft area to be made ready for the painting.

'The bell was tolling but Robert would not let himself hear it.'

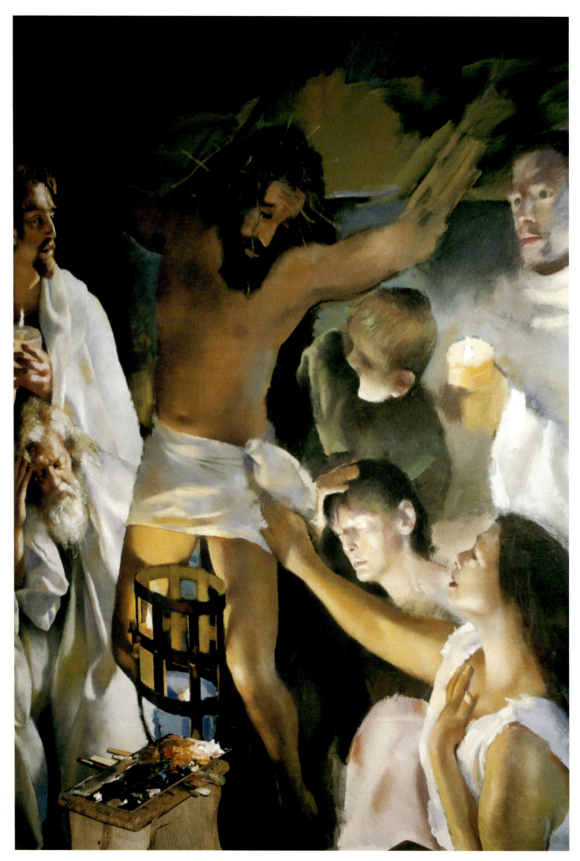

The Crucifixion.
Author's note – this painting was being worked on in such a small studio area that it was impossible to stand back far enough to capture the whole painting.

competitive in social situations using his knowledge of philosophy and art history like dazzling swordplay. But it was in his pursuit of scale that Robert's competitive nature showed up most. He clearly felt a need to be well out in front of the rest of us with his 3000 sexual partners, 10 000 paintings and 250 000 book collection. He would mention an early painting that was, he claimed, 360 feet long and told me once that he had planned to create a mile-long painting on Dartmoor. Then there was the dreamed of new development on the Barbican to accommodate the Lenkiewicz collection in total. This was to have the largest circular stained glass window in England. People would gasp. The thing of scale and numbers was a consistent feature in Robert's thought. In general terms it is difficult to construe this feature as anything other than the pursuit of competitive achievement – the opposition had to be outclassed. There is an obvious degree of immaturity in all this, of course, but then competitiveness is a form of immaturity, constantly seeking attention, that is.

Overall then, the picture is of an exceptionally creative and talented man who conformed to the stereotype of the coronary prone personality. In my view his coronary prone behaviour pattern inevitably contributed to his death. One might also speculate that a number of the creative people in the survey carried out by Jaques may have been just like Robert in combining an unrelenting, torrential creativity with a denial of health risk, in other words, coronary prone personalities. Maybe some of those suffering early death died of coronary heart disease and not of a depressive decline following a mid life crisis as Jaques suggests? Set against this, as Jaques would predict, when Robert did make the time to paint from his heart there was, latterly, a much more reflective style and tragic theme – as with his Last Supper and The Crucifixion.

As a final note on my assertion that Robert was a fine example of the coronary prone personality I must report my experience at a recent auction of Robert's paintings and artefacts.

NOTES

20 October 2004

I have just returned from a private viewing for a further auction of Robert's paintings, drawing and artefacts. I have stayed very conscious of the paragraphs above that I wrote last night. Bearnes, the auctioneers, achieved an impressive standard in setting out the items for the auction to create what, in the event, became the best art exhibition in town. The lighting, arrangement and general atmosphere was most impressive. The viewing was in an enormous function area and comprised some 613 lots, a large proportion of them being paintings. Because the numbers of people present were manageable and the layout and setting spacious it was possible to stand back and take the whole thing in as one exhibit, rather than 613 items. Again I am struck by the sheer scale of Robert's productivity; one scans round and thinks 'just one man has done all this, incredible, he must never have stopped - yet it is less than a tenth of his overall output.' I have no sense of wavering from my categorisation of Robert as a coronary prone personality – here was the bold evidence. One of the more obvious features was that a large proportion, probably over half, but I did not count, of the 178 true oils are not finished. There is the sense of the painter rushing on to the next interest. It takes me back to the point I made at the beginning of the book. Robert had an addiction to black canvases and an addiction to setting out a painting on these. What he lacked, though, was an addiction to finishing them. Perhaps this is fortunate because it would have run him off his feet.

Small sections of the Bearne's auction display.

Early INFLUENCES

FAMILY AND SCHOOL – *Interview with John Lenkiewicz*

It would be presumptuous of me to make any claim of a proper analysis or formulation of the psychodynamics that helped maintain Robert's behaviour. I just did not have the type of relationship with him that led to methodical analysis. What I intend to offer instead are some building blocks towards an eventual formulation that may slowly accrue over the next decade or so from a variety of sources.

A central feature that must be accounted for is why the appeal to throw out established order and seek an independent path in life resonated so strongly with Robert. It has to be a complex answer and I can only give fragments. At a very basic level genetics will have played a part. He was born with an exceptional aptitude to sense and then reproduce in paint the visual array before him. He was vastly more capable than most of us before he even started his training in painting technique – it came naturally. With this grew a 'torrential creativity', that is, a mind buzzing with ideas and creative projects. To such a person normal family life, normal social life and normal school in London in the fifties and sixties must have seemed suffocating. In his autobiography he writes of having moved between the two worlds of brutish schooling and the unhinged ravings of his parents' environment (Hotel Shemtov). It is relevant, therefore to take a brief look at the environment and type of relationships that shaped Robert's development. He gives much graphic detail in his autobiography but some of the stories test one's sense of credibility a little. For example he records tending to the dead inmates of Hotel Shemtov from his early teens on and even of witnessing a resident's death through 'projectile' haemorrhage from about every orifice and surface organ on the body. He told me and also records in his book that he remembers his father as a dour, incommunicative character who only ever spoke to him once. His mother he described as a neurotic woman who favoured him but pushed him forward to do the tasks in the hotel that she did not like – such as dealing with deaths among the residents. To achieve a balanced view I have sought an account from another member of the Lenkiewicz family to put things into some perspective.

I had for some while been hoping to meet with Robert's younger brother, John, who regularly travels to Plymouth for meetings of the Lenkiewicz Foundation board of directors. John trained in biophysics and bioengineering and for some years served as a consultant gerontologist, researching the biology of ageing. During the past twenty years, though, he retrained and set up the Institute of Sexuality and Human Relations in London, which he now runs.

NOTES
An Interview with John Lenkiewicz
9 November 2004

We met late in the afternoon and spent an hour and a half together in The Crown and Anchor on the Barbican. Although I have never met John before, it was curiously nostalgic since John bears a facial resemblance to Robert and has a very similar manner of speech and laugh. One felt one was within the Lenkiewicz domain once more. We quickly fell to talking about the early family atmosphere and circumstances that will have influenced Robert. There were three boys in the family, Robert with his twin brother, Bernard, and John who was younger by two and a half years. John wanted to stress that his memory was no more to be trusted than anyone else's but, at the same time, did feel that some of Robert's personal history told in his autobiography may have been subject to a degree of reconstruction.

Mr Isaac Lenkiewicz, in John's experience, was not the incommunicative and rather forbidding presence that Robert described. Rather, he was an amiable, quiet, rather sweet man. He had been a horse trader in Germany and, of great interest to John, recent contact with his eighty-three-year-old first cousin, living in Argentina, revealed that Isaac Lenkiewicz had two main interests in life, 'smoking and women'. I started to think in terms of Robert's emphasis on sexual activity and the possibility of genetic links here. It seems that part of Isaac's reason for fleeing Germany with the rise of the Nazis was linked to a relationship with a non-Jewish 'Aryan' woman. This, the 'racial crime' was forbidden under the 1935 Nuremburg laws. John felt disinclined to speculate in depth on the influence that Isaac may have had on Robert partly because of the overshadowing dominance of Mrs Lenkiewicz.

From John's picture of his mother, Mrs Alice Lenkiewicz could be described as the opposite of her husband. As a therapist he thought that the two formal diagnostic descriptors that best suited her were 'histrionic' and 'narcissistic'. She was a 'power house of a woman', an absolute workhorse. For some years, she ran Hotel Shemtov virtually single-handed, coping with the cooking, cleaning and organisation and even dealing with residents who presented trying problems such as double incontinence, illness and death. Clearly Alice imposed a work ethic of the 'coronary prone personality' type upon herself and will have modelled this to the boys, at least, if not instilled it in them. Maids were engaged when finances permitted but the work ethic prevailed. As a presence, John remembers her as having cultural affectations (tracking back to a relationship with a blind antiquarian in her younger days). That led to many anecdotes and pretensions concerning concerts and literary experiences. She would read philosophy to her blind companion and from this early experience conveyed the philosophical atmosphere into the household with regular mention of key philosophers to the boys – again a habit that was evident in Robert. However, Alice was prone to being very loud, very forceful and reacting with histrionic shrieks and dramatic acting out when events did not go her way. It is a memory of both John and Robert that, throughout the day or at the meal table, Mrs Lenkiewicz could suddenly become very upset over a trivial issue and flee the house with great drama and noise to end up sitting on a bench around the corner. One of the three boys would then set off to find, placate and comfort her and ease her back into the house.

Robert's relationship with his mother, John believes, was intense and entangled. She held Robert in idealised high regard and, in a broad sense of the word, was in love with Robert. It is not clear that Robert enjoyed this attention and special place because their relationship was rather tempestuous and he left the house aged 17 to quite wound Mrs Lenkiewicz by the infrequency of his return visits home.

Alice Lenkiewicz in death – the face.

Their father died aged 60 when the children were all quite young but, even so, on the occasion of his death when he collapsed in his bedroom, Mrs Lenkiewicz shrieked loudly and Robert and Bernard were summoned to the bedroom to help lift their dead father back on to the bed. Mrs Lenkiewicz died later, aged 78, and John confirmed that both he and Robert did visit the hospital and did view the dead Mrs Lenkiewicz. Robert swept away her cover and her body was revealed wrapped in a cellophane bandage with her head and her toes bound exactly in the manner that Robert reproduces in his sketches of the event, the portrait of his dead mother and his own Death Scene (see below).

Alice Lenkiewicz in death – the body.

As far as the Hotel Shemtov goes, it seems that very few of the residents were actually victims of the Holocaust (though a couple of the cooks certainly were), nor had they fled to avoid it as Robert sometimes suggests. They were mainly elderly Jewish residents, some British but mainly from pre-war Eastern Europe. There was a steady death rate at the Hotel but John was very sceptical about Robert's stories that he was sent to wash the bodies of dead residents and also his dramatic story that he held the hand of one resident while she haemorrhaged to death. Sceptical in the sense that Alice was very capable and domineering and just dealt with these things as a matter of course. As for the stories that Robert had his first sexual experience at the age of 11 and the first attempt at intercourse at the age of 14, both with a maid, John knew of no details but thought this quite feasible.

In general, the boys seemed to have the relationships typical of brothers with the usual incidents of squabbling and conflict. All three of them experienced bullying at school, often of an anti-Semitic type. John remembers little physical bullying but was certainly subject to a continual atmosphere of menace and the threat of physical bullying when at secondary level, although not necessarily anti-Semitic (Robert has described to me incidents when his head was pushed into a toilet and the toilet flushed and how he was held underneath a dripping icicle). A degree of asymmetry was introduced between the brothers in the sense that Robert and Bernard ended up at a Secondary Modern school whereas John went to a Grammar School and then to the University of Manchester and University College. He eventually trained in sex therapy at St George's Medical School. I asked John if Robert's initial trailing at education, given that he was a very intelligent lad, was more to do with the bullying than intellectual capability. Being quite young at the time that all this went on, he had no relevant memories and was unable to confirm this one way or the other.

Turning to the present day, I asked John about his general view of Robert and he summarised this as saying that he recognised that Robert has been an enormous influence in his life and that he has always been hugely impressed by him. He is very admiring of Robert's prodigious achievements but, at the same time, critical of elements of his lifestyle. Inevitably I asked him how convinced he was of the claim concerning 3000 sexual partners. Diplomatically, John replied:

JL: 'It isn't impossible, though perhaps he simply used 3000 as a coded way of saying, 'a huge number.' But it was an important characteristic that Robert was completely fearless concerning transgressions of conventions or moral codes.'

Concerning the women involved he believed encounters with Robert 'left a good proportion of the women feeling that the lack of exclusivity in their relationship with Robert was painful,' and that 'this will not have escaped Robert's awareness at any level'. I asked if he thought the whole thing of sexual profligacy might include an element of unconscious attack on women driven perhaps by an unconscious attack or retribution towards the dominance of his mother. We discussed this for a while and came to the conclusion that it was possible but there just isn't enough background information to confirm or deny it. At the same time, it is clear to us both that Robert was truly and genuinely attracted to and fascinated by women.

John is familiar with Robert's health record and noted that he sustained an attack of viral endocarditis about 15 years ago that would have damaged his heart and later received a relatively rare quintuple bypass to reverse advancing coronary heart disease. These bypass vessels were, however, also blocking up quite seriously in the last year or two of his life.

We concluded with, what for me, is a key question:

KN: 'If Robert's sexual excesses and incessant work drive were to be construed as manic defences then what are the defences against?'
JL: 'If anything, they were defences against death and oblivion. He was very attached to life.'

John's reply took me by surprise in view of Robert's pronouncements to me that he was inured to death, having been exposed to the atmosphere of illness and death both in the hotel and with the vagrants in his refuges. He went so far as to say to me that he welcomed his own death commenting, 'What suits a blade of grass suits me'. John's observation suggests that this might have been a pronouncement based on an idealised notion of his. We had a brief email exchange concerning this and John replied:

JL: 'Here too, I feel there is a misunderstanding. I would be surprised if Robert ever said, or meant to say, he welcomed death. Certainly, he was fascinated by it, constantly referencing it in his work. He also surrounded himself in the iconography of death (skulls, tombstones, coffins) and studied many aspects of it in depth. I feel Robert was more accepting of death than looking forward to it. He often said towards the end of his life that he'd 'lived the lives of ten men'. This is undoubtedly true.

EARLY INFLUENCES – PHILOSOPHY

As John Lenkiewicz noted, the Lenkiewicz household tended to be rich in the names of philosophers, with references to them and relevant quotes being voiced by Alice Lenkiewicz from time to time. Clearly this had a real impact on Robert since so much of his attention and thinking related to mainstream philosophers, with Nietzsche taking pride of place, perhaps, in his thoughts. It is certainly not accurate to say that Nietzsche was everything to

Robert but I do want to argue that the writings of this nineteenth century philosopher did have a very significant and enduring impact on Robert's approach to life. Nietzsche set himself against the teachings of his German society. He strove to construct a new order in an endeavour that has been described as the systematic destruction of systems. He wrote of man and society after the 'death of God' because he saw the very notion of God as stultifying society and denying truth. He urged people to strive for self-mastery and independence through the pursuit of knowledge and independence of thought – 'find your own way' was the call, implying an abandonment of the church. In his writing he created an heroic figure in the form of a hermit like monk who endured a cold, mountainous wilderness for years before finally descending to dispense his thoughts and wisdom. This took Nietzsche to his crescendo, his concept of 'obermensch' which means overcoming. The idea is one of transcending our very selves in the quest for self mastery and finding an independent pathway devoid of God. He sought a new order of values and morals for society.

Robert wrote that 'at eleven Rembrandt climbed up, at twelve Michelangelo and at thirteen Nietzsche'. As shown earlier, the watercolour linked to this statement shows Lenkiewicz with these three on his shoulders while he is bowed under their weight. He talks of reading Nietzsche a great deal when young and often refers to Nietzsche's writing and thoughts. It is easy to find parallels that suggest a true influence of Nietzsche in Robert's life. In particular, Robert adopted a deconstructionist stance to the near-universal contemporary conventions of male–female relating and parenting, effectively condemning these as a form of fascism. He set himself against broader conventions within our society, choosing at times the social isolation brought about by living among vagrants. He clearly pursued his own version of 'obermensch'. He sought to establish his independent view of life having turned away from any religion and also broken away from the constraining power of official and social disapproval. In some ways it might be said that Robert role played Nietzsche. His inclination to solitary thought and writing (of which he did a lot), his earlier abrasive independence of thought, values and behavioural code – even the way he opened himself to be influenced by music. For Nietzsche it was Wagner and his operas, for Lenkiewicz it was Mahler who provided part of the inspiration for the paintings Dancing with Mahler, and The Burial of John Kynance. Louise Courtnell has commented that Robert was especially passionate about opera.

A similar case might be made concerning Robert and Albert Schweitzer or contemporary deconstructionist philosophers such as Derrida. These too figured in Robert's thoughts. But, basically the general point is made and I haven't the heart for any more on philosophy at this particular point.

A PERSONAL VIEW ON THE PSYCHODYNAMICS OF ROBERT LENKIEWICZ

I have noted before that I did not have a formal relationship with Robert as his therapist and so the following is, of course, quite speculative in nature. Each and every one of us is influenced and shaped by our early experiences in life, with parents playing a particularly important part in this process as it interacts with genetically controlled features. Robert was no different. He was born with a sharp intelligence and an early ability to absorb the advanced thinking of philosophers and the skills and vision of great painters. Not that it would have shown in the earliest of years but he was also born with a very powerful sex drive. He had a natural talent for painting that quickly evolved into a distinctive and appealing figurative style – even in adolescence. His talent was quickly recognised by his mother. Her powerful presence and emotional attachment to him made her admiration and approval very potent in shaping Robert's behaviour. He became the 'little king', perhaps, within his mother's world. Early on he learned that his 'gifts' as a painter and quasi philosopher were a means of opening doors to special status and hence a general indulgence of his eccentricity and whim.

This charisma-based bonding Robert would later transfer to many other devoted women, but his mother will have been the first and most formative of such experiences. Alice Lenkiewicz will, however, have probably been such an intense presence that Robert found it stifling and, for the adolescent male unbearable. As a result he acquired a need to distance himself from overbearing emotional attachment. Here was the origin of a classic emotional conflict. The early experience of devoted admiration and love from his mother left a permanent need to be the object of such focused attention and affection *but* this conflicted with rebellious feelings against the stifling and controlling dominance that came with it. Hence the lifelong need to fight free of possessiveness and control by women. At the same time his focus of interest *was* women rather than fellow males and male activity. Thus, since leaving home, Robert has always created a situation where he was supported and freely indulged by loving and admiring women. He sought women out as a means of replacing his mother's devotion and attention but, as the years passed, he tended to disperse the emotional pull and possessiveness of women by creating a multiplicity of relationships, most of which were held at a distance. The potential power of the women on whom he depended was 'defused' by his secretiveness and his knowledge that he was continually celebrating freedom through new relationships and sexual partners.

Robert's rare skill and talent as a painter and his presence as an intellect and sociological guru imparted a sense of greatness that resulted in him never needing to search for relationships, in the main they presented themselves to him. This built a robust self-confidence. At the same time it became an entrenched pattern to create situations where women had little real power over him.

The experience of anti-Semitic bullying probably caused Robert to turn away from his male peer group and seek the easier world of solitary creativity and reading. This led increasingly to a pattern of assertive absorption in his own projects, his own thinking and his distinctive creativity which, early on, was probably a form of retreat. It was a reply to the rejection at school and a response to the admiring approval of his mother. Later, rather than a retreat, this pattern became a device for self-confirmation and self-promotion.

The early adventures in Hotel Shemtov were sexually disinhibiting and also had a formative impact in terms of exposure to tragedy, philosophy, age and death. Sex thus became a joyous, guilt-free addiction while tragedy in one form or another became his inspiration. His eccentric involvement with philosophy and the philosophical circle (at age seventeen) further shaped his thinking and gave him permission to live out an interpretation of the deconstructionist approach of philosophers such as Nietzsche, that is, he went his own way, rejecting convention and creating his own moral code and values. Acceptance with this group, which he revered, came by way of his painting skills and the orientation towards philosophy that was gained from his mother. Painting, philosophy, individualism and eccentricity were thus 'locked in'. Being very well read in the history of art and the biographies of great painters there will inevitably have been some modelling on these lifestyles. He talked of Courbet, Gericault, Da Vinci, Michelangelo and Raphael as models. It was not just lifestyle but these figures will also have encouraged Robert toward scale and numbers. He talked once of the fantasy of Courbet in his studio 'surrounded by paintings' – the exact atmosphere that Robert created in his various studios.

Speculatively, I suggest that John, the younger brother, simply by his presence became a threat and competitor for Robert's position in the family in early days. Later, of course, there was John's success in formal academic terms (attendance at a Grammar School while Robert endured a lowly Secondary Modern school), and his progression into university and postgraduate research. This will have provoked the defensive competitive element in Robert that is sometimes found in the oldest child of a family who, having been 'infant king' for a while, finds the threat of being displaced made real by the arrival of a younger sibling. It is no surprise that, as a young man, Robert was thrilled by and set out to emulate the large scale paintings of the French romantics – the attention commanding scale and power of, for example, Gericault's 'The Raft of The Medusa'. His account of his reaction to such paintings suggest that they resonated with his need to know that he could continue to command attention. In this way *his painting also became a device for competing – with its emphasis on scale and numbers and, above all else, passionate quality.* It is also relevant to note that, as a young person, Robert recalled being moved and inspired by Charles Laughton's romantic film of Rembrandt's life history, noting that he ended life as a beggar. As he told the story to me it was as if the character of Rembrandt in this film had conveyed a personal message to him saying, 'be like me.' The character involved seemed to fit Robert's emotional needs at the time and he seems to have embraced the vision.

Robert will have quickly discovered that his conscience-free eccentricity and sexual profligacy was another means of distinctiveness and, therefore, of competing. Whether the early sense of quest that he talked of was, in reality, a habit that reflected the early striving to achieve unassailable dominance in the competition for an unrivalled position in the family is something for discussion. 'Quite possibly' would be my answer. Combined with this

Robert's mother also modelled and, no doubt, will have preached the importance of an unrelenting work drive. Usually exposure to such parents instils a guilt if one is not tirelessly productive.

Robert's views on the harshness of society were influenced at an early age by involvement with the residents of Hotel Shemtov. It is noticeable that Robert continued his contact with the dispossessed in his long-running involvement with vagrants and alcoholics, again as if holding on to something from his early days. Lastly, the seeds of his downfall perhaps, his passion for rare, old books again echoes the memories and values of his mother and the nostalgic values of the older residents and members of the philosophy circle. As Robert once said, 'You can smell the past in the books.' This love led to an unfettered acquisitiveness that rested on the lifelong assumption of continuing indulgence. But the indulgence began to run out and the potential to become our greatest living painter was put at risk by the distractions of dealing with reality (debt).

Putting it all together it is possible to see the once-in-a-century combination of quite exceptional painting skills, brimming creativity, unusual intellectual influences and a powerful intelligence all fortuitously combined with family dynamics that maximised the expression of these features. The family dynamics also led to an outlook and set of values that freed Robert to behave in relation to whim while driven by a powerful sexual interest, together with a relentless work drive and competitive energy. It made for the exceptional Lenkiewicz legacy that is, sadly, being slowly dispersed as I write.

Robert AND ILLNESS ROBERT AND DEATH

Robert was in and out of hospital a fair amount in his last ten years. He suffered a viral infection of the heart, advancing heart failure, acute appendicitis and gout. As I have described, his attitude towards his health was, in my terms, cavalier. In his eyes his body was a device for forging ahead with his quest. It was not something to respect and service (through rest and exercise) or conserve. When illness did intrude Robert happily brought his drama and charisma into the situation. I visited him a few times when he was in hospital in Plymouth and there was an evident Lenkiewiczian pantomime element about it all. The staff were clearly subject to his charms and there was no doubt that they felt that they were nursing a great man worthy of special status. He was protectively set aside in a side room and actively sheltered from unwanted or intrusive visitors. Probably some of this atmosphere of a 'special patient' was generated by Robert's conversion of his room into a temporary studio, with various paintings cluttering the room, while the wearing of a dramatic white gown (no striped pyjamas for Robert Lenkiewicz) enhanced the scene. He did paint quite a bit when in hospital and recorded his own entries into diary-style notes and watercolours. A typical extract comes from notes at the top of one watercolour:

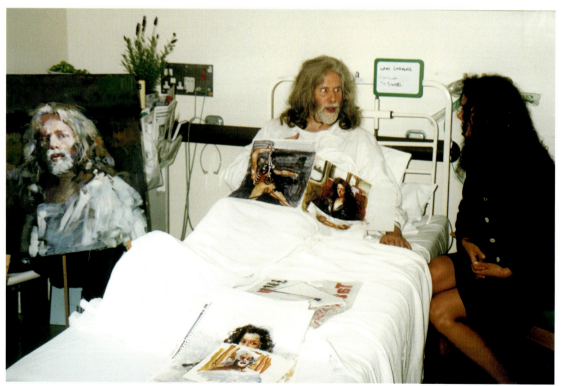

The hospital room became a kind of studio— Anna Navas is the visitor.

Six male doctors, all charming and confidence boosting – 'Let's listen to your chest again'… (more on painting)… 'Yes excellent – mumble, mumble – frusemide – mumble, mumble… Yes, Yes now let's listen to a good cough' (more on another painting). 'Yes excellent, have we discussed discharge…?

Visitors to Robert's room in the hospital tended to reflect the pattern of visitors to his Basement studio. On the occasions when I was there a steady stream of female visitors filed in and then out or waited patiently for their personal time slot.

I have mentioned on occasions throughout the book that Robert's style was to drive himself relentlessly in casual disregard of his health. His response to episodes of illness seemed to be a curious mix of optimistic denial and the theatricality of being an invalid. I phoned him shortly after his appendectomy and he said that he was fine with 'absolutely no ill effects at all', and so he planned to do several hours work at the main studio the next day. In reality, having phoned Yana the next day to book a meeting, she said that he had turned up at the studio but was pale and weak and, after fiddling around ineffectually for half an hour, he disappeared off, obviously not feeling too bright.

At one level Robert knew that he was fading and that his heart had a limited time left before something like a heart transplant was needed. He had been quite weak at one point but he responded unusually well when his cardiologists fell back on an old drug for heart failure called digoxin. This perked things up for a year or so until problems with fibrillation (bursts of fast, irregular, incompetent heart beats) started to show up. During this period he did not spontaneously talk of illness or death but if asked would recognise that he was on the slide. This was reflected in some of his work, particularly an unfinished painting that he described to me as a depiction of personal time running out. It is a self-portrait with the unusual feature of 'pushing an hour glass into my mouth'.

Robert had prepared for death in one sense. He had painted his death scene under the title Self Portrait – Death Bed. It is a lovely painting of a romanticised event with some of his close partners and children gathered around his dead body. The depiction shows the chin bound by a cloth and the toes tied together – just as he sketched his mother's corpse when viewing it at the hospital.

'Hospital notes'.

Detail of a self portrait during a stay at Derriford Hospital.

Robert in his personal room in the new studio – a watercolour of the 'Hour Glass' painting is seen on the adjacent bed (January 2002).

The Painter with Hour Glass (unfinished).

Robert lent me his notebook of preparatory readings, notes and watercolours for this painting for a while, and yet again I found myself humbled in a sense. His research, his commentary on the research, his creative energy combined with his sense of personal drama do set him aside as someone quite exceptional, so very intellectual, such stature. Some watercolours from the notes are reproduced here with one or two comments, together with images from the Death Bed itself. Reflecting on death did not seem to lift Robert's spirits. On one page of notes Robert writes rather enigmatically:

I am dead – surrounded by my slaves and progeny. It is only a matter of time before they are all dead. My seminations force all that I am ultimately deprived of to take the same just sentence. They will all die – with or without my pride.

Rather less dark, perhaps, but still somewhat sombre:

To have my gang weep over me so lyrically and get away with it could only happen in Hollywood or Memphis. I simply do not arouse such passion.

This is a rather interesting misperception. Robert's commemorative event in Plymouth was full of tears, memories and lyricism; a fine production in fact. Ironically, Hollywood in style I thought.

Alice Lenkiewicz in death (watercolour in Death Bed notes)

As often happens, when the influences to Robert's products are investigated, old favourites come up in the notes. In this case the derivatives feature Courbet and Rembrandt and, maybe less of a regular, Munch. He records the events of Courbet's death as seen, I assume, through the doctor's eyes:

> *He then made this sadly all-too-true remark, 'I think I won't live through the night'. And he repeated the words to the men who watched at his side… He woke up towards 10pm and stayed for some time in a sort of somnolence. He said a few words then lost consciousness. The death pangs began towards 5.a.m. and lasted a little more than half an hour. Courbet died at 6.30.*

This scene is converted into the fanciful image shown in his Death Bed. Robert is surrounded by women who were important to him at the time. They sadly watch the parting of his spirit while children wait or sleep at the foot of the bed. As it happens, the manner of Robert's death will have irritated him grossly. It was the opposite of dramatic theatre – an uncomplicated, solitary death. Robert was simply found dead in the downstairs room of a small house in Plymouth one summer morning. He had been sleeping in that room on his own. Of course, as might be expected with Lenkiewicz, there has been controversy about the nature of his death with some voices claiming that he need never have died had he been taken to an emergency unit that day. In contrast Annie Hill-Smith noted that, although Robert had been quite poorly for a week or two, partly because of a new medication, when she saw him on the day before his death he was rather better and had a normal colour back in his face.

As a last word on this theme, and to provide a link with the next section that highlights Robert's debt problem, it is worth noting that Robert wrote of the debt that beset Courbet prior to his death. Again one becomes aware that Robert steered his life along similar pathways to that of his much admired idols. In the Death Bed notes he wrote regarding Courbet:

> *It was the last day of 1877. The next day the first instalment of the indemnity would have fallen due; and once it was paid he would have been free to return to Ornans and Paris… A few weeks later, being a very poor man and overwhelmed by the death of his wife and child, he asked Regis to pay his expenses (272 francs), Regis refused.*

Knowing what I did about the state of Robert's heart and his enduring coronary prone behaviour pattern, I should have placed a sizeable bet on his premature death. It was inevitable really. Up until the end I did occasionally try to interest him in the obvious threat of his relentless work drive causing further exhaustion and strain to his already failing heart. As always it was a futile exercise. Robert would simply smile at me in a distant, tolerant way

The corpse of St. Bonaventura displayed (watercolour in Death Bed notes)

'To have my gang weep over me so lyrically' (watercolour in Death Bed notes)

Self Portrait – Death Bed (indication of size)

Detail: Self Portrait – Death Bed

156

and, if anything, strive to work faster and harder. I would give up and just watch the show. He once said to me regarding his own death, 'I regard it as a sweet oblivion, I welcome it.' I suspect, though, that he actually found it very inconvenient, especially in relation to the grandiose plans that he had been formulating concerning developments in the Barbican and his ambition to reduce his debt and save his library.

DEBTS, STRAIN, CRISIS AND COLLAPSE

One disappointment that people sometimes express about the overall character of Robert's more recent work is that there is much routine repetition at the expense of substantial works. He spent much energy producing a seemingly endless sequence of portraits, often of young women. Many of these are best described as average examples at best, unremarkable when compared with the depth and talent that he sometimes displayed. It was something of a puzzle to me when I visited the Basement studio to encounter an atmosphere akin to a production line with dozens and dozens of such paintings littering the rooms.

Robert discussed different things with different people. I never asked about his financial situation and he did not raise the topic frequently. However, he did venture to confide in Michael Palmer on some of the financial pressures in his life. This is helpful material in accounting for why Project 20 (Addiction) seemed to have been virtually abandoned and why so much of his time in the two or three years before his death went into work of limited substance. I am grateful to Mike in contributing the following notes on his link with Robert and bringing to light the rather stark financial situation that almost certainly contributed to Robert's physical collapse and death.

The production line

The Decline of the Painter – The Experiences of *Michael Palmer*

My relationship with Robert began in 1985 while working at the ABC cinema in Plymouth. As the 'house manager' I soon became aware of this unusual man as a regular film goer. Our first conversations were brief, concentrating on films and my work. A few months after I first met him, Robert invited me to his main Barbican studio and I vividly remember that cold and wet November day. I felt nervous on entering the building, moving through the small passageway leading to the creaky stairs. At that point I was overcome with the feeling that 'something special' had happened to me as the main room of the studio came into view. I imagined that I'd gone back in time and was visiting the great painter, Rembrandt. It was an exciting and uplifting moment, but so unexpected. At the top of the stairs I stood still, transfixed by the quantity of paintings displayed all around. Sheepishly I called Robert's name and, from a distance, he beckoned me to enter. As I approached him at work, his easel and large canvas gave way to Robert's gentle smile and, to my utter embarrassment, that of a beautiful nude girl, sitting on his lap, having her portrait painted! He told me to pull up a stool and, in response, retaining an air of indifference at the sight before me, I remained absorbed there for nearly 30 minutes, quietly chatting to him while he painted.

Throughout the 16 years I visited Robert, my life became a much richer one because he was so interesting to be with, especially when we were on our own. From 1999 to Robert's death in 2002, I saw him on average twice a week and most Sunday evenings I'd meet Robert at the Basement studio, his 'secret activity centre'. All types of people and interesting characters visited 'the basement' to do business with him.

When Robert was in good health, he was able to turn out small oil canvases of pretty young girls in a couple of hours and would sell them on for £1000 to £2000 a time. He was able to produce over twenty a week besides undertaking his major projects and an enormous amount of other private work. For Robert and I, Sunday evenings became a time when we'd just talk for an hour or so, relax and reflect on the week just passed. Once a month he would gather up all the paper bags from shelves and cupboards hidden around the tiny, three-roomed studio and count up the money. Sometimes he needed to find £30 000 to £40 000 to pay off debt. This would then be shared out to the book dealers and a variety of other associates, including his many assorted helpers and various beneficiaries that Robert felt obliged to help. Money was handed out to all types of people and for all sorts of reasons. He often paid the house rent and bills for several of his female sitters and had even bought property for some. There were also a couple of girls he sponsored throughout their university studies and others who always persuaded him to part with cash for an 'emergency' or 'crisis'. And an enormous amount of money was spent on artefacts which Robert collected to display within his newly converted Theology Centre which was to become his main exhibition and study centre. Any other funds left over went to all and sundry who'd just happen to ask for a handout, like the street people who needed money for their next fix or drink. It was understandable why Robert never had any cash in his pockets. In spite of his reckless generosity, he believed that he could pay off his entire debt of nearly £500 000 by the end of 2002, so long as he did not buy any more rare books which, of course, he always did. But, remarkably, he was well on course in achieving this goal only months before his death.

Occasionally, but especially if he had been ill, Robert would become desperate for money to pay off his creditors or to purchase something he couldn't pass up. Of course, he could raise more funds by doing another deal with one of the loan sharks or dealers but he knew that the spiral of debt would become more complicated if he did. So I'd sometimes offer him my own money and, through me, he bought several items, from religious artefacts from Papua New Guinea to a clock owned by Aleister Crowley. He was, however, always embarrassed by this situation but, to me, it was a simple arrangement which caused no financial difficulty and, anyway, I was just happy to help out, as friends do.

He always had ongoing business deals and I found it incredible that most of these secret arrangements were secured with only a verbal agreement and consisted of a simple contract between Robert and his creditor. It took the form that if Robert didn't raise the required sum each month to pay off his debt then an expensive painting would have to be given as a holding guarantee to the person involved. The paintings offered were supposed to be held as security and given back when full payment was made but, unfortunately on many occasions the creditors would not return the work, which infuriated Robert. However, he'd never force the issue and would just say to me that he felt trapped and unable to do anything about it as he didn't want his cover blown. His greatest fear was of being caught out and he suffered greatly as a consequence. During the last two years of Robert's life, he painted more and more for the dealers and the other people who hounded him for payment and so, inevitably, his private projects and known ventures were having to take a back seat. However, he maintained a busy regime right to the end of his life and was still able to produce a self portrait series, watercolours and still life work besides the large portraits which he worked on at the Theology Building.

I was privileged to have been painted by Robert six times and, indeed, felt honoured to have portrayed St Andrew in what I believe to be a masterpiece, The Last Supper. Sadly, it was not completed but still it remains a breathtaking example of his absolute genius.

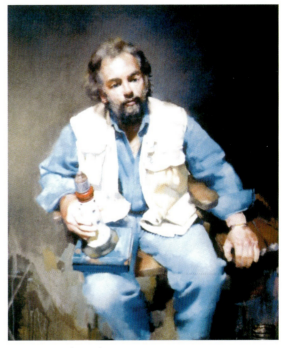

Portrait Mike Palmer.

Robert's only consuming passion in his life was for his books. He put his incredible book collection before anything else. Even the 'erotic note book project' came a poor second to his enthusiasm for improving his remarkable library, which is probably the best of its type in Europe and covers such diverse subjects as literature, metaphysics and poetry to religion and art. He once told me that he would rather do time in prison than lose any of these precious books and, of course, he had already served time at Her Majesty's pleasure, which he hated.

Throughout the hours I spent in his company, I found Robert to be a happy and contented man and he would tell me that he, 'knew of no-one who enjoyed such a full and rich lifestyle,' as he did and that he was grateful to do so in the knowledge that he was not being a nuisance to others. With hindsight, perhaps his unconventional lifestyle and the excesses were brought about due to his ill health and his genuine belief that he would die within a short time. In fact, in 1997 he gave himself only another four years of life.

The press caused Robert great concern during with their inaccurate stories about him. Although he was a great showman and self-publicist, nevertheless he was always fearful of being exposed and caught out, whether it was by the tax man over his dealings or related to his erotic note book sessions. He simply didn't want to upset or disappoint those closest to him and that is why he was so very secretive, but remarkably organised, in everything he did.

The ladies that he painted, sometimes ten in a day, provided an endless discovery for his work, although naively he could never understand what they saw in him. Beautiful girls and older women were besotted with Robert and most happily threw themselves into his sexual forays for the 'erotic enquiry project' which involved over 3000 individuals and had spanned 30 years. Although this sexual experimentation was always misinterpreted in the press, I did, in the end, genuinely believe his motives for undertaking such a unique and vast project which meant so much to him as an artist. His own sexual activity declined markedly towards the end of his life although he found other ways to continue with this project, by diversifying his sexual techniques, to retain a meaningful and worthwhile relationship with each of the individuals that he courted.

Robert did not fear death but he knew that there was only a short time left to him and so he pushed himself every day in everything he did. He would sleep no more than perhaps three hours a night then paint almost continuously at every opportunity.

At the end of 2001 and at the beginning of 2002, Robert's health deteriorated rapidly, accelerated by the pressure he was put under by a few individuals who wanted paintings or payment. There was no let up to these demands put upon him and sometimes he would be completely exhausted from it, becoming desperate in just trying to keep his life together. But his illness meant that he could no longer produce the quantity of work he needed to meet his financial commitments and this, too, caused him even greater distress. At this time, he suffered from three separate burglaries, when many pictures were taken although, for Robert, it was not so much the loss of these paintings that upset him but the time it had taken to create them. Time was very quickly running out for him. Indeed, during the last year of his life he produced a series of works entitled 'Man Swallowing Hourglass' which depicted Robert holding an hourglass to his mouth. In continuous ill health, he often told me that he felt as though he was drowning when sleeping which, in fact, was caused by fluid on his lungs. But he would never say anything or make a fuss and just carried on, slowly becoming weaker as time slipped away. During his last stay in hospital, Robert stated that he nearly admitted everything to key figures but then decided that he could cope a little longer and so made more unreasonable deals on the telephone from his hospital bed just to buy himself extra time, to sort things out.

Robert believed in small kindnesses as they were an important part of his life and he helped many charities. He actually owned very little himself, had few clothes and did not drive, drink or smoke but absorbed everything around him. He accepted human frailties and indiscretions as normal behaviour, allowing himself not to judge others. He was a very caring man, although perhaps not in a conventional way, and he had a wicked sense of honour. He was also a great storyteller but, most of all, loved living his life. Every now and again he could seem naïve, sometimes he'd exaggerate and, occasionally, be contradictory. For my part, I will always treasure the laughter we shared together, of the vulnerability I saw in him, especially in his efforts not to get caught in compromising situations, and in his desire not to upset and disappoint the people who mattered to him. He knew that, after his death, those closest to him would initially see him as a 'dirty lying whore' (his words, not mine) but believed that after six months he would be forgiven and, perhaps, even understood.

    I saw Robert at his home during July of 2002 and, although bedridden, he still remained optimistic. I last spoke with him on the phone a few days before his death and he seemed very weak but resigned to whatever was to come. We made arrangements to meet. Shortly after Robert died, I visited him as he lay in the chapel of rest but it was a sad experience for me. His spirit had gone and his waxy, embalmed form was a million miles away from the warm- hearted Robert I had recently spent time with.

Michael Palmer, April 2003

The END OF THE SHOW

FAREWELL TO A MAN THAT I WOULD NOT HAVE MISSED

Robert had some difficult ways and I cannot claim to have been an unconditional admirer. But I was unconditionally fascinated by him and miss him greatly. The energy, the relentless creativity, the scheming, the breathtaking knowledge of how oily substances may be used to represent visual array and encompass a compelling depth of human meaning and feeling, the sheer profligacy of his consumption of sexual experience, the skill in composing environments to evoke intense interest and theatre, the dramatic personal presence, the breadth of his knowledge on philosophical, religious and fanatical thought, his mastery of the history of art, the childlike enthusiasms and offbeat humour, the addictive behaviour pattern and associated devious activities, the exploitative traits, the entrancing and engaging persona, the curious mix of charm, caring and near psychopathic disregard for the feelings of women, the exaggeration, the unrealistic but thrilling visions for future developments and his ability to make people feel that it was important to be important to Robert Lenkiewicz, remain as a complex eidetic image in my awareness. There is no doubt whatsoever, it was a magnificent show. It was unrivalled in my experience and, with it now ended, I am aware of an emptiness to a part of my life that is unlikely to be filled again. He was, simply, unique – a man that I would not have missed. Which means that I miss him now. Not just him, though, but the atmosphere he created. To walk into a studio or room that Robert used regularly, even if he was not there, was to encounter the literal look, feel and smell of the distant past. Combined with the compelling interest provoked by all the paintings, articles, books, furniture and artefacts found within, it would give an experience rich in fascination. I really do miss these environments.

If Robert's death was at an inconvenient time for him it is only fair to note that he was not the only one to be pitched into unexpected inconvenience. If he was a consummate showman in life then he certainly did not abrogate this role in death. Even as I write this, some two years after his death, the drama is still intense. With his 'alternative economics', his secretiveness and the compartmentalisation with which he managed the various elements of his life, he has managed to leave a financial mess that, one might say, has a dramatic and surreal impact equivalent to some of his best paintings. He has surely left broken hearts, too, since the apparent failure of his loyalty to those who sought only to support and promote him must have been deeply wounding. Annie Hill-Smith, until very recently the chairman of the

Lenkiewicz Foundation (a charity that has striven to establish a Lenkiewicz Centre to formalise the presentation of Robert's paintings) told me that she had tried repeatedly to persuade Robert to make a formal assignment of a number of his paintings for The Foundation, the intention being that it might have a basis on which it could survive and establish itself. He would decline in the short term, insisting that this was indeed his intention but that nothing was available at the time. In fact, nothing was available, it seems, because he was doing exactly such a deal with various booksellers to defray new debts following new book purchases. It is public knowledge now that, on his death, the Foundation actually owned very few paintings outright but was destined to wait until the settlement of the estate to receive the paintings that remained. So began the last great Lenkiewiczian drama, since it also soon became public knowledge that Robert's estate, although of a magnitude to be measured in millions, had a crushing series of debts and liabilities set against it. Worse, the Lenkiewicz Foundation would only be a recipient of paintings if the estate was finally able to emerge solvent. The outcome of this critical issue of solvency has yet to be resolved.

Annie Hill-Smith, chairman of the Lenkiewicz Foundation until November 2004.

At the centre of the drama is Robert's executor, Peter Walmsley of Boyce Hatton, Solicitors in Torquay. Having been Robert's solicitor and friend for many years, Peter's task is unenviable. Not the least reason being that Robert eschewed paper records and invested heavily in verbal agreements for unrecorded deals. In many instances deals had been made that related to the costs for newly acquired premises, work undertaken on these, or books purchased, all to be set against paintings – many of which he had not handed over, finished or even started at the time of his death. Verifying claims on the estate, assessing the inevitable counter claims, legitimate liabilities and debts must be the stuff of migraines. It must also be a sadness for the executor progressively to have to break up and dispose of the estate's collection of paintings and books at various auctions in order to settle claims. Not the least problem being, one infers from press releases, that as the number of claims steadily expanded the value of the estate seemed to recede, in part because the book collection fell short of its anticipated value.

Robert did have a bit of a thing about witchcraft and demonic forces. This would sometimes show up in small inserts in certain paintings and in the books and artefacts that he collected. He also, it is now known, was not as reliable as he might have been in his communications with the Inland Revenue. As Peter Walmsley remarked to me 'As executor I have a legal duty to finalise the deceased's tax affairs for the period up to his death.' It is certain, therefore, as the final acts in the post-death financial drama now approach, that were Robert still alive and able to produce a tableau to represent the drama of the settlement of his estate the Inland Revenue and their colleagues from Customs and Excise who deal with VAT would quite inevitably be depicted as a demonic presence lurking behind his artistic quest. This might be unkind perhaps since, if anything, they may judge themselves to be the aggrieved party,

Peter Walmsley, Robert's executor.

Robert with his 'devil' machine.

The Prophecy.

burdened by a devil in the form of a painter. On a visit to the Theology Building Robert demonstrated his devil machine. A simple mechanism raises a demonic figure behind a gravestone. I said 'Who is the Devil?' He replied, 'Oh, let's say the tax officer.'

One of Robert's recent paintings perfectly catches the current mood amongst the 'Lenkiewicz Circle' to the extent that I feel it merits the name, The Prophecy. My interpretation of this painting may not match Robert's but he would strongly approve of that as an example of how the viewer sees only his own projections, not those of the painter, when viewing a painting. Anna, representing all the people that were close to Robert, sits in sad repose embracing a self-portrait of Robert. In the small self-portrait he is clothed in an almost ghostly white gown, depicted as a diminished and fainter presence. He is in a place without features and holds a small book – perhaps his book for the day of the Last Judgement that he wrote about so eloquently. When I saw this painting a year or two before his death it struck me as a painting that held an intentional prophesy. It announced in clear terms (although not necessarily at a conscious level) his recognition of his approaching absence. The painting now symbolises the experience of many of us who had links with him, we embrace the inanimate remains but the vibrant life and spirit of Robert Lenkiewicz has gone.

INTO THE POST LENKIEWICZ ERA

A colleague once asked me, 'Have you lost your presence of mind, how can he have such appeal?' Hopefully this book will have served as a long answer to that question. In truth, I actually found Robert to be quite personally disturbing at one level because in his thinking and much of his behaviour he often seemed to function as if entirely ungoverned by conventional rules – social, interpersonal, financial or sexual. He lived out personal impulse much more so than anyone else that I have met. Inevitably then, his experience of life was, in some ways, immensely rich and colourful compared with the average citizen, such as myself. I freely confess that this provoked a sort of ethereal envy such that every time I left him it felt like I was returning to a real but colourless world full of rules and inhibitions that make life orderly but stiflingly dull at times. Having said that, more than one Robert Lenkiewicz at a time might become something of trial, perhaps.

It is noticeable that, after a funeral service, the body of people assembled at the subsequent wake slowly get louder and more removed from the key event of the day. Eventually the atmosphere is infused with a happier feeling of it being time to go. There may even be reassuring platitudes along the lines of, 'Well, there it is, he's gone, time to move on'. Not all find this easy in Robert's case but letting go has to be achieved. Preserving what is important and idiosyncratic about Robert Lenkiewicz is essential, but we do have to get used to the fact that he is gone now. Hopefully the current tide of dispersal of his creations and collections will soon ease and some of his paintings together with some of his notes and writing will be collected together and made more generally available.

Echoes remain, though, that will not go away. I notice these days that when I visit exhibitions of paintings, I often view in the spirit of one pursuing a quiet, somewhat sad search for another Lenkiewicz or, at least, someone who Robert might find to be a kindred spirit in lifestyle and someone who can paint with a talent that has the potential to match his own. It is good to be able to end on a positive note and reveal that it is not a futile search. It has been a great encouragement to find some of his most talented pupils producing paintings that clearly belong to the Lenkiewicz school. The ongoing portrait work of Louise Courtnell and Yana Trevail, for example.

As for the kindred male spirit element, that search has not been futile either. Recently, at the Delamore Arts annual exhibition in Devon, a painting, Woman Emerging from the Shadows by Max Lowry, stood out to me with an immediacy that felt a little similar to my first reactions to Lenkiewicz paintings. The 'chemistry thing'. Max is, it transpires, a young painter currently working in London, with a lifestyle (I discover) that has definite commonalties with Robert's. His father's people were Russian, Max being brought up by his Northern Irish mother. With an Arts degree from Royal Holloway, London University, he paints with energy and passion and, perhaps, the hint of a Russian darkness that I found appealing. He is influenced by the Impressionists, Degas in particular, and also by the Masters, Da Vinci and Michelangelo, that is. He spent much time in his youth in Paris where he regularly wandered in the galleries. I enjoyed learning of his childhood artistic adventures that, again, had echoes of Robert's background:

Robert is gone – his ever-open studio now barred.

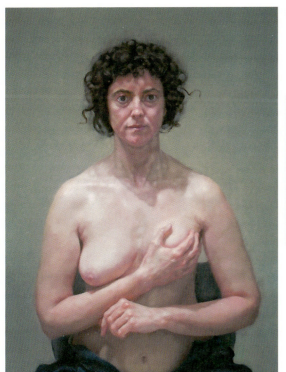

Intimate Self Portrait (Louise Courtnell).

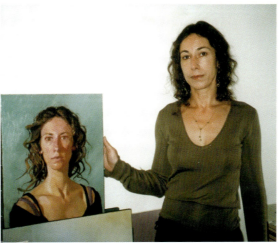

Self portrait (Yana Trevail).

A section of Max Lowry's mural in London.

NOTES
Friday 5 November 2004

My mother, who has always encouraged my creative activities, even gave me a wall (as an open canvas) in her first flat in London, where I was born. The wall ran the length of the corridor to the front door and I spent thousands of hours reworking the space, until the flat was sold some years later. My mother, thinking it might help push the sale through, wallpapered the corridor – to the horror of the buyer, who immediately stripped it back to my work – it remains there to this day.

There are curious parallels in Robert's and Max's common tastes for figurative painting with women sitters and in the extension of the painter-sitter relationship into a closer personal event. It is also the case that Max has worked on (and completed) a significant mural commission in London. Not, perhaps, on the scale of Robert's Round Room at Port Eliot but significant, nevertheless. Were Robert still alive I think that he would encourage and support Max and see him as a man to whom he could relate and so pass on the task of maintaining the hallmark of Lenkiewicz. This distinctive mark gives special focus to the celebration of the female form while keeping alive the skills and themes of classical figurative painting in contemporary England. A charismatic male presence is, of course, also part of the required 'aesthetic package'. The examples of paintings by Max together with those of Louise and Yana given above state some of my hopes for the post Lenkiewicz era:

Woman emerging from the shadows.

Max Lowry at work.

Sirens (Lowry).

Farewell Robert